The Drums of War

"A man should not be inarticulate just because he is dead."
—T.C.C. journal, Dec. 7, 1951

The Drums of War
Copyright © 2018–2023 by the heirs of Thomas Cyril Corbett,
except as noted. Used with permission.
All world rights reserved

Compilation and introductory commentary
Copyright © 2023 William A. Corbett
All world rights reserved

No part of this book may be reproduced, stored in a retrieval system, or transmitted in any form or by any means electronic, mechanical, photocopying, recording or otherwise, without the prior consent of the editor, William A. Corbett.

Readers are encouraged to go to www.MissionPointPress.com to contact the author or to find information on how to buy this book in bulk at a discounted rate.

Published by Mission Point Press
2554 Chandler Rd.
Traverse City, MI 49696
(231) 421-9513
www.MissionPointPress.com

Book design by Sarah Meiers

ISBN:
978-1-958363-72-0 (Softcover)
978-1-958363-71-3 (Hardcover)

Library of Congress Control Number:
2023903215 (Softcover)
2023903215 (Hardcover)

Printed in the United States of America

CY CORBETT CHRONICLES

The Drums of War

An Autobiography
by T.C. Corbett, 1917-1924

The Corbett family at 6318 Greenwood Avenue, 1918.
(Left to right): Thomas Harold Corbett (Buster) and dog Spot,
Elizabeth Corbett, Marie Corbett, Thomas Cyril Corbett,
Theresa "Aunty" Keenan.
(Courtesy of T.C. Corbett Family Archives)

WILLIAM A. CORBETT
EDITOR

MISSION POINT PRESS

Contents

About Cy Corbett Chronicles. vii
Introduction ix
Editor's Note About Style and Syntax xiv
Acknowledgments. xv
Preface. xvi

Part One: Before My Departure 1

One: War, War, Grim-Visaged War 3
Two: My Visit to the Walsh Home 10
Three: Farewell Parties Begin. 16

Part Two: I Am Summoned to the War 33

Four: Ground School 35
Five: 1923 Pilgrimage 48
Six: Pilot Training. 58
Seven: The Sickening Sound of Silence 74
Eight: The Good Companion. 87
Nine: Texas Twilight 108
Ten: Army Journalism. 132
Eleven: The End of the War. 142

Part Three: Returning from the War 153

Twelve: You Can't Go Home Again 155
Thirteen: The Death Vigil 168
Fourteen: Job Hopping to the *Tribune*............ 179
Fifteen: Newspaper Life 186
Sixteen: Aftermath of a Crash 193
Seventeen: End of Drums....................... 199

Cy Corbett's Cast of Characters 204
About the Author 224
About the Editor.............................. 226

About Cy Corbett Chronicles

My father, Thomas Cyril Corbett, was—to put it mildly—an eccentric. He was born in 1895 and died in 1976. By 1912 he had taught himself Morse code and communicated with ships on the Great Lakes. In 1918 he piloted Army biplanes fifteen years after the Wright brothers made their historic flight, and then Cy lived to see man land on the moon and return safely. The fact that man had progressed technologically so quickly in one lifetime simply amazed him.

Cy Corbett Chronicles is basically a serialized autobiography. As editor, I have assembled his various writings and attempted to put together works of interest to an audience beyond members of our immediate family. You will learn about the life of my father from several sources: journals he intermittently kept from 1916 through his death; the Greenwood Avenue stories he wrote in the early 1970s; a novel he kept revising over a thirty-year period; and letters and other writings, including a partially-finished history of his alma mater—St. Ignatius College (now Loyola University)—and various vignettes he wrote from time to time.

Following the Great War (WWI), Cy was honorably discharged from the fledgling US Army Air Corps. He worked in a variety of jobs, finally landing at the *Chicago Tribune* in 1921 as a copywriter and editor. After nearly twenty-five years he resigned and moved to Michigan. He built a small summer resort on six and a half acres overlooking the big lake. The revenue from summer vacationers helped him live and send his kids to college. And in the off-season, he wrote.

Introduction

The title for this work, *The Drums of War*, was chosen by Cy Corbett himself, who used this phrase and variations of it in his later writings.

After our mother's death in 1981, the family divided personal effects among the three surviving sons. I received the bulk of Cy's personal journals and papers, and my brother Tom took various scrapbooks, albums, photographs, and a couple of the journals. I began my work transcribing the Greenwood Avenue stories shortly thereafter, and later the journals themselves. Tom, a working anesthesiologist, reviewed Cy's material when he could find the time. He especially enjoyed scanning old pictures and negatives.

A few years ago Tom turned over to me Cy's original scrapbook that included small photographic prints of his army days, as well as his time at St. Ignatius College. I reviewed carefully all the material he had, and consolidated relevant parts into my assemblage of Cy's writings. Nowhere could I find any reference as to why Cy had chosen the title, *The Drums of War*. I did, however, find a piece entitled "The End of Drums," which is included in this manuscript.

When the draft of this current volume was nearly complete, Tom and his wife visited us in northern Michigan. My sister-in-law Beverly related the following incident. One day many years ago, while cleaning up Tom's desk, she ran across a scrapbook with a piece handwritten in pencil on aged, lined notebook paper. It was old and faded, and held together by discolored Scotch tape. It was pasted in one of Cy's scrapbooks among a few wedding announcements of old friends.

"As I remember it," Bev explained, "your father described lying on his army cot in the barracks, resting. In the distance he could hear drums beating. They signified that a soldier had died, and the procession was escorting the body to a hearse, or perhaps a train. He could tell by the number of the drums and their loudness whether it was one body or two that was leaving the base." She said the piece evoked strong emotions and was so moving that she remembered it in great detail all these years later. She conjectured that it was so personal that perhaps Cy had decided not to use it in his recollections written for public view.

Try as we could, reviewing again the fragile scrapbook that held pictures and announcements during Cy's army years, and the red journals that had been in Tom's possession, we could not locate that particular piece of writing.

I thank Beverly for sharing the incident. It may well explain how Cy chose the title of this work.

In today's terms, it might be said that Cy suffered from post-traumatic stress disorder, but back then, it was more commonly known as "shell shock." However, Cy never made it to the Front, so his condition was probably overlooked by the many physicians he visited. In reading his notes we learn, however, that the death rate among cadets learning to fly was actually higher than for the pilots at the Front. So, seeing many of his comrades die or become seriously injured may have actually induced a form of trauma, aggravated by his early propensity toward melancholy. Further, he suffered an abdominal injury in one severe crash. It continued to bother him his whole life.

Cy was active in the Air Service Reserve from his discharge in 1919 until 1936. In the summer of 1929 he spent two weeks on active duty at Selfridge Field, Mount Clemens, Michigan, where he was qualified to solo in the new trainer ships. Several times during his later years he mentioned that he gave up flying in the 1930s because Lady Luck had sent him an unmistakable message. He was scheduled for one of his weekend Air Service Reserve flights in Chicago, but had to cancel because he had been called into work at the *Tribune*.

Henry C. Sandusky, the pilot he was to fly with, was assigned another copilot, Lt. Charles H. Fargo. Later that day they crashed into a brick house at 124 East 75th Street, on Chicago's South Side. Both men aboard were killed. The fatal flight was Saturday, April 30, 1932. Cy was thirty-six at the time. An inquest ruled that the cause of the crash was because of an "accidental closing of a carburetor mixing valve." Sandusky was thirty-five; Fargo was thirty-three.

The only comment we could find on the incident was in a recollection, written two years after the fact, in a journal entry dated August 23, 1934:

"From the minute I heard of his death, Saturday evening, for several days I felt like a dead man myself. It was a strange sensation. The Air Service meeting was scheduled for Monday evening following the tragic Saturday. After work that night I drove up to the Press Club where a place was set for Sandy, and his empty chair drawn up. I felt like his spirit was there. I got beautifully tight on Air Service punch."

In an upcoming volume of his biography, *The Tribune Years*, we will learn of continuing health struggles and Cy's attempts to overcome them. In 1920 he was diagnosed with "intense mental depression." Although Cy didn't immediately follow his doctor's advice to spend at least a year working outside (he took a job at the *Journal of Commerce* and later at the *Chicago Tribune*), in 1921 he built a getaway lake house in Indiana, an hour's train ride away. Further, in an effort to ease his "mental trauma" while in the city, he kept an outside garden. Later, after moving to Michigan, he spent much time outdoors creating a summer resort with beautiful rose gardens adorned with elegant Roman, Greek, and Italian statuary.

Throughout his life, Cy kept himself busy in attempts to keep the "Irish Melancholy" at bay. During more leisure times, he turned to writing as a panacea. His journals were his outlet to vent, tell stories, and relate what life was like for him, hoping that someday a son, or grandchild, or even a stranger might explore his work and see it published. I've come across several notes of instruction while assembling his writings, suggesting placement of various pieces and giving background information. It appears that he always had confidence that someday, someone would eventually discover his writings.

As Cy said in many ways and several times, "A man should not be inarticulate just because he is dead."

By 1917 the war in Europe was heating up and it was becoming evident that the United States would soon become involved. President Wilson convinced Congress to pass a declaration of war in April, and shortly thereafter the Selective Service Act was enacted.

There emerged a nervousness among the ranks of college men, and great discussions ensued on the morality of our country's potential involvement in the Great War. Further, there was anxiety about the chance of being conscripted. The topic came up during conversations at parties, in classes at school, and in private thoughts. Cy Corbett's diary, *Journal of My College Days*, captured many of these.

In the midst of war talk, Cy was becoming bored with school and felt that serving either in the radio corps (he knew Morse code and had obtained his radio license in 1914) or the Aviation Corps would set him above the general ranks. Further in the back of his mind, he was looking for a way to prove his worthiness to a girl who had held his fascination during the previous five years. (That story is told in another volume of *Cy Corbett Chronicles.*) So, in September 1917 he submitted an application to join the Army Air Corps.

The contemporaneous entries from *Journal of My College Days* gives us a taste of life prior to entering the army. Cy ceased entries in that journal upon leaving for ground school in

November 1917, but resumed them after his discharge in 1919. He later wrote various reflections about his service, and in 1923 returned to Texas and Love Field, prompting him to write *Pilgrimage*, a reflection on his years in the service. In December 1925 sections from *Pilgrimage* were printed in *The Little Trib*, the in-house publication for employees of the *Chicago Tribune*. In the introduction to the piece, "Lady Luck—Be With Yo' Baby," *The Trib* noted:

> On Friday Morning December 12 and again on the following morning, Cy read parts of his book into the 'mike' of W-G-N, The *Tribune*'s radio station. Readers of *The Trib*, we are sure, will find the chapter we have reprinted from his book just as entertaining as the excerpts he read were to the immense radio audience.

Going through Cy Corbett's journals and papers, we found a draft of the unpublished *Pilgrimage*, and have incorporated it into this volume. Further, we've supplemented the text with pictures from Cy's archives, and outside sources as well, in an attempt to give a clearer picture of what he experienced during the Great War years.

While awaiting the call, Cy became confident that his premonitions were more accurate than not. He had convinced himself that his fate was to die in the war, heroically. We can see from his prewar journal that he consulted several Jesuit friends, and he was finally put to ease that if he did die serving his country, the afterlife would be kind to him.

His premonition of an early death, however, was dead wrong. He lived to age eighty.

When my father died, he didn't leave us a million dollars. But he did leave us a million words.

—W.A. Corbett

Editor's Note About Style and Syntax

Cy Corbett adopted the style used for years by the *Chicago Tribune*, abbreviating certain words to save space, when each line had to be created in lead by a Linotype machine. Hence, he would abbreviate the word "through" as "thru." These stylistic idiosyncrasies are scattered throughout this work. A further convention of the time: instead of using dashes (—), Cy would use a comma and a dash (, -). Where I thought appropriate, I have retained his original style.

Also, because of my personal interest in genealogy, I have left intact various names Cy mentions in his journals, though many people were only incidental to his main story. Occasionally, I have added footnotes providing biographical details on individuals mentioned. I've also listed the names in the "Cy Corbett's Cast of Characters" section at the end of this volume. It may be of some help to those seeking information on their ancestors.

Acknowledgments

Thomas Henry Corbett, MD (1938–), for scanning all the negatives and photos left by TCC, and providing insight and editorial guidance.

Transcriptionists and typists: Marcie McKinley, Bill Prichard, Bill Moulton, and Nelly Heitman. And Roseanne McKinley, for editing.

Thomas Harold Corbett (1904–1973) for helping Cy Corbett remember the early years of Greenwood Avenue while sitting on a rustic swing overlooking Lake Michigan.

Readers of early drafts: Stephan Julius, Thomas Henry Corbett, Charlie Holden-Corbett.

My thanks to all for helping in this project, in whatever capacity you could contribute.

—W.A. Corbett

PREFACE
by T.C. Corbett

November 11, 1968

Fifty years ago today, I was a singularly innocent and unperceptive very young lieutenant in the Air Corps with my wings and roughly 300 hours in the air. I had no idea of what lay ahead of me, firmly believing it would all be good and glamorous. I had no idea I would be alive in fifty years, and little did I realize that those days would be the highlight of my life. By then, unknown to me at the time, something had already broken the back of my daring and initiative, and confidence in life.

There are things I can still remember that would have been well worth a record. A trip with Requa (a civilian instructor, a Frenchman and in mufti, a beau exquisite), during which we flew twenty-five feet over a railroad train and dove down across its path, only a little ahead of the engine.

There was Cecil Dodge, captain, and excellent flyer. I flew with him one day and met him the next day in the hospital. We both had the flu.[1] For ten days, we occupied adjoining cots and lay there talking the long day away. He was one of the most interesting men I have known.

And there was a young lady whom I met at the Country Club. Her secret ambition was to have a plane come over her house and stunt for her. We arranged it for a Friday evening, I remember, for about 8 o'clock, just as it was dusk so that I would not be seen by the authorities at Love Field. I flew over Highland Park, picked out her house and stunted for five minutes—everything I knew how to do. I stunted from 3,000 down to 700 feet. Thinking I had given her the thrill of a lifetime, I returned to

---

[1] The Spanish flu of 1918–20 killed an estimated half-million people in the United States and fifty million worldwide—more than all the casualties of World War One.

the Field and called her up. She was not at home, her grandfather said, but he had seen the show and enjoyed it very much!

And there was one glorious evening I remember. Through the soft dusk the Texas sun went down, splashing the whole landscape with opal and azure, and the air itself, as I looked down to the ground, seemed a solid lavender mass. It was soft and warm and my motor was hitting perfectly in a ship that responded to the slightest rudder. I landed, then considered that it was too pleasant to go in. So I took off, intending to go around the field once more. I went around twenty times, landing each time before the plane came to a stop, giving her the gun, and ascending again. It was perfect. I never felt so at one with a ship. I felt as the birds must feel as they wheel around in the dusk, the glory of motion, the glory of color, and the whistling of the wires and the soft caress of the Texas night. The lights were twinkling in the hangars and I could no longer distinguish where the air left off and the ground began. But finally I had to pancake down and taxi the ship across that silent field to the hangars.

In the comparative serenity of old age, passions spent, vision cleared, and ego deflated, it is much easier to write about a life than it was to live it. How good a writing job we do depends on how well the old mind-computer has borne the years. And on how truthful our instinct was in the first place.

Ego is probably the worst enemy of Biography. But in old age it is beaten down by the numerous defeats of life, and we can see things more truly, more in proper perspective than ever before. Probably why the best pictures of life in ancient Rome were given us by men almost senile, -Seneca, Sallust, etc.

The writer can always say, "I hope this is truthful. At any rate this is how it appears to me now." And that is about as close as literature can ever get to Truth in the Past, particularly if we bring to the reading our own grain of salt. And that is what everyone does.

I must acknowledge and give thanks for many promptings and suggestions from somewhere. Psychologists will say they were from my own subconscious mind, but I don't think so. Rather I feel they are from interested parties in the great sea of souls around us.

And so I hope you may get something out of this awkward account of America in the early years of the Twentieth Century, written for his charming little grandson by a nobody who had nothing to gain by bending the truth one way or another.

Presented below is a summary of service written shortly after my discharge in 1919.

Chronology of Service in the Air Corps:

I served for fifteen months in the United States Air Service. I applied for acceptance to the Air Service in September 1917. November 24, 1917, I was sent to the University of Illinois Ground School from which I was honorably graduated February 4, 1918.

I was stationed at the Air Service Concentration Camp, Camp Dick, Dallas, Texas, from February 6th to March 1st, 1918. From March 1st to August 14th I received training as a flying cadet at Love Field, Dallas, Texas. August 14th, 1918, I was commissioned as a second lieutenant pilot in the Regular Army.

From August 14th to November 4th, 1918, I completed my advanced training as a war pilot, specializing in aerial gunnery, acrobatics and combat work. Other courses included: Navigation (aerial); theory and practice of Engines; army paperwork and Tactics; construction and operation of all types of machine guns; Aero Dynamics and the theory of flight, practical study of the construction and assembling of the airplane; Aerial Photography; Artillery Reconnaissance and Infantry Liaison.

November 4th my training was deemed complete and I was ordered overseas with the 56th Handley Page Aero Squadron to Mitchell Field, Long Island. We then assembled at Roosevelt Field, Mineola, Long Island, where I was assigned to the 149th Squadron, 1st Provisional Wing. But before the Squadron embarked, the Armistice was signed and overseas orders were countermanded. I served at Roosevelt Field until Feb. 4, 1919, on which date I was honorably discharged as "a loyal and efficient officer."

While in the army, after the date of my commission and prior to my being ordered overseas, I edited an eight-page camp newspaper, *The Love Field Loops*, at the behest of Major G.S. O'Connell, acting adjutant. This work was done in addition to and without diminution of my work of flying and taking eight academic subjects necessary to complete mastery of the art of flying.

I carried on this work conscientiously until one day while in the air I fell into a spin three times, narrowly missing death in the last one. When I came down, I was ordered to the hospital and examined. The doctor said that I was "out of condition and developing a fast heart" due to the strain of excessive overwork. He ordered me to the hospital for a rest. After I was there a week my overseas orders came through and I succeeded in persuading him to let me go.

PART ONE:

Before My Departure

ONE

WAR, WAR, GRIM-VISAGED WAR

Journal Entry: April 5, 1917 (Holy Thursday)

 Tonight the United States is at war with Germany. At 3 o'clock this morning the house passed the resolution 213 to 50, and at 1:11 this afternoon the President signed the war proclamation. Last night the Senate passed the war resolution 82 to 6. It looks as though I may be a soldier in a short while. It seems the President intends to get 500,000 men by drafting, if necessary.

 Two days ago, after I saw in a paper the notice of the conscription act, I felt as tho my fate were sealed. I felt instinctively all day that I would die on the battlefield or in the trenches. But going to Communion this morning at St. Ignatius relieved the pessimistic mood. Don't misinterpret me. I think I am not totally craven—I would fight and die for the country that gave me birth and liberty and the privilege of an education, if her life were endangered. But this seems to me to be fighting for her old enemy, Britain, -and in a strange land. I seem to be a fatalist and a pessimist. Oh, the Glamor, the Glory, and the Misery of War.

April 6, 1917 (Good Friday)
　　Was at church, today, at 3 o'clock. Church again this evening. Met Dorothy Lyons and Joe McCormick. We talked about the war. Dorothy abhorred it. Joe said he was a pacifist. Just last month I received an invitation from the government to join the radio corps in case of war. I certainly could see a lot of action as wireless operator on a submarine chaser.

　　My friend Toots Weisenburger is afraid that my knowledge of wireless will cause me to be drafted. Toots's brother Irving is joining the army and leaves in a few days. After Confession last Wednesday, I had Fr. Coppens bless beads for Irving to take with him.

　　Mother, of course, is worried about the war. My friend Sherwin Murphy and I discussed his job and the war and his desire to join the Officer's Reserve Corps. Despite the war talk, we enjoyed ourselves only as two old friends can.

April 7, 1917, Saturday, 9:00 a.m. (the last day of Lent)
　　Ed Colnon and Tom Walsh arrived in Ed's big Packard. We drove for about an hour. Ed is thinking of joining the aviation corps. He is qualified—he drove 40 miles an hour part of the way!

A potpourri of various journal entries, April-September 1917:

　　The senior class is thinking of getting in the Officers' Reserve Corps. Walsh proposed that if the case were urgent, we (ourselves) get a petition to go to school all summer and up to November, probably, and get our degree first in case we have to go to war, for two reasons.
　　1. We would never, after the war, come back to finish.
　　2. As college graduates, we could get in the Officers' Reserve Corps.

On May 31st I took a walk in the evening. Trees rustled just like they did in South Haven. Brought back old scenes, old faces and old memories. Before I go to war I would like to write something that would live. I often feel inspired, but when I come to write, the inspiration deserts me.

Sat on a bench for a while. I occupied myself with thots of how I would settle up my few affairs before going to war. I would select from my library appropriate books as mementos for each of my friends:

Ned	New Testament in Greek & Latin
Earl	Macaulay's Essays.
Toots	Don Quixote
Mother	My book of verse
Buster	Henry Esmond

I would also write a letter to each, and to all my old "profs": Frs. Lomasney, Magivney, McGuiry, Garvy, Leahey. I would also write one other letter whose purport I will not here disclose. I would put them all in a large envelope, seal it and mark it not to be opened until I am reported dead or missing. I would trust it in Toots's care and appoint him my executor. If I came back I would receive the sealed envelope and burn it.

The "Draft" came to pass today (Friday, July 20, 1917). So far the numbers of none of my friends nor of myself have been called. It started at 9:30 this morning. I worked calmly till noon, ate my dinner, called up home—nothing definite—and went back to work again. The only time that I felt anxious was after work, scanning the numbers in the paper.

I have been drafted. Today (Thursday, August 9, 1917). I took the physical examination. The folks feel very bad. I am too stunned to say anything. Tonight, I suffered an agony of mind which I have experienced seldom if ever before. I will do my duty as God gives me to see it, cost what it may. I am consoled by this thot and by the assurance that there is a God, a law of right and wrong, and a higher power over men than mere chance. This is not a herding of sheep to the slaughter, the strong driving its weak to their will; or, at least, I like to think that it is not. I hate to fight beside England's red rag; but I would die for the Stars and Stripes, for home and fireside, if necessity demands.

The notice came yesterday as a bolt from the clear sky, just as Aunty, Marie and Bus were ready to start for South Haven. Their trip was called off.

Tom Sheehan, an old school friend of mine, told me on the way to work that he thot that I should try to get in the Radio Dept. of the navy. I called up Jim Shane, who is in the naval reserves. He took me down in his auto after work, and I think that I can still get in. I called up Vincent Cunningham[2] and told him about it.

On Friday (August 10, 1917) I got over to St. Ignatius for my 9:15 a.m. date with Mr. Schmidt. I told him that I thot it incumbent on a man of education to inquire into this thing before entering it. We talked about the Justice and necessity of the war, and he assured me that I was perfectly justified in entering. He spoke of duty, of the uncertainty of life and of the fact that life is very insignificant in the face of eternity. He has soothed my mind and calmed my spirit. Now I feel resigned, even buoyant. I feel that whatever happens is in the knowledge and the care of God.

On Saturday (August 11, 1917) Mother called me up while I was at work and told me that she had just found out that I didn't pass the physical examination, so I was refused. She is so relieved—she seems, as I told her, ten years younger. I guess I

---

2 Vincent Cunningham was a classmate at St. Ignatius College who eventually married Cy's sister, Marie.

was about 12–15 pounds underweight. I thank God for it and yet I want to do what is my duty.

Sunday was a day of rejoicing at our house, on account of my being exempted from army service. Mother and I sent over to the office tonight to find out what further was to be done.

We learned that I was not exempted at all, that I had actually passed the physical examination. Mother cried bitterly and nearly fainted. We came home and told Aunty. We all cried, Mother and Aunty to have me go, and I to leave them and all that was dear to me.

Aunty went back to find out more. While she was gone, I told Mother what I have never told another mortal. I wanted no secrets between us when I go. I told her that I loved Sis Walsh, and that it had broken my heart when she left South Haven five years ago. Mother was very sorry that I had never said anything about it. Why didn't I? In the first place, I was shy. I never wrote to her because my honor was delicate on that point. She was rich and I was comparatively poor. Now, I have no secrets from Mother, or from this diary. I feel better. Come what may, I shall meet it with calmness and with fortitude.

Friday, September 7, 1917

Went to Communion this morning. Received a letter from Rob Walsh inviting me down to St. Louis in the most friendly terms. Found out today that I may go into training sometime in October.

Monday, September 10, 1917

This diary, which is a very curious document, is fast drawing to a close. Curious? It is half diary and half novel. As a novel it seems to be approaching the crisis and the climax. In it I have half hinted at what has occupied my thots for a long time. And now the climax is about to top it all. I wonder what the denouement will be?

I have to tell my little story. I have been silent with the diary lately, tho I have had much to write about, but little inclination to write. Now the sluice gates of my tongue are loosed and naught can stop me. The hopes, fears, ambitions that have possessed me, a student, are now about to end.

I had dear, dreamy old South Haven to write about and did not, in fact, could not. I have had much to write about in the matter of my joining the army. I have had farewell letters, but couldn't. I wanted to edit this diary, but I couldn't. I don't know whether there is yet time to do all that—I don't care. The one supreme thing is going to happen—next to death, the one great adventure of my life—I am going to St. Louis!

Army, my ambition to write, everything I know of fades into insignificance beside this. It is as if an angel from heaven came and offered to take me by the hand and lead me thru the realms of Paradise, -I have been cold. I have been cold for years. I have schooled myself to be deliberate and unemotional that I might in more patience await this day. God, how I have dreamt of it.

As I write I think of Father Lomasney. He knows me, understands me, as only a man can. He knows that I have been a dreamer, an idealist—that I have tried to be as honorable as Henry Esmond.

Three influences have molded my life and character, and have occupied my thoughts. I name them in the order in which they came. The Greek Goddess (Sis Walsh), my Jesuit education, and Henry Esmond. Next to my Mother I love them most of all earthly things. They have been near to my heart. Sis I have never forgotten, the bright-eyed little fairy. (I was struck by the poetry of it.) For the advantage of a Jesuit education, I thank God for one of the rarest privileges granted to men. I have met noble men, holy and saintly men; idealists that are not to be found in the world. No matter what the world has ever thot of the Jesuits, I will vouch for their integrity and sanctity with my honor, and I have loved it more than life.

I am delirious tonight. You who may read these lines, I wonder if you know what this time means to me. Life is slipping from me. It is but a matter of days till I enter the army. That is the denouement. The crisis—St. Louis. Yes, I am like other men, cherishing the same hopes and fears. I wonder if she will know me.

I wrote Rob today and told him I would arrive in St. Louis at 5:57 p.m. Thursday, Sept. 13. I can hardly realize it. I wrote to Ned Reynolds[3] also, saying I would like to see him Sunday next.

When I think of the five years just passed I think that with sufficient provocation, incentive or vocation, should I say, I could be a saint, patiently going thru the years like Father Coppens, far from his native land and all that the world holds dear. When he heard of the destruction of Belgium he wept bitterly, it is said.

Whatever the army holds for me I shall take calmly for it is only the denouement.

Thursday till Sunday I shall live thru *The Log of an Argonaut*, tho I will feel little inclined to write it. Writing has sunk to a trifling business.

I think with Clinton Scollard—

"In the clatter of the train
There's a lovely, small refrain—
I shall see my love again!"

---

3   Ned Reynolds was a childhood friend from Woodlawn who joined the Jesuits and was studying in Florissant, Missouri, not far from St. Louis.

TWO

My Visit to the Walsh Home

I THINK OF THE COUNTLESS NIGHTS I have wandered the darkened streets of Woodlawn, after studying late, trying to get rid of the old longing that is an ache. I have watched the leviathans of steam and iron halting for a moment at the 63rd Street station on the Illinois Central before their long rush thru the night to St. Louis. I dreamt of the day I would be on one to see Sis Walsh again.

Thursday, Sept. 13th, I left home and family for St. Louis, having been invited there by my old friend Rob Walsh. I left at 10:17 a.m. from 63rd Street on the Illinois Central. Mother and Marie saw me off.

The day passed more or less uneventfully. I went into the smoking car, smoked a great many cigarettes, read a little of *The Saturday Evening Post*, and was very nervous, especially as we were pulling into St. Louis.

The train stopped about 6 o'clock. I got off and walked down between the long rows of coaches, but there was no Rob in sight. I came to the gates, went thru and out onto the street. No sight of Rob. I came back into the station after a bit, intending to go to the waiting room when I spied Rob coming. I was very glad to see him, and so was he, apparently. He is a most matter-of-fact and unemotional fellow. He looks a great deal as he always did: pompadour, a rather artistic face, tall and well filled out.

He carried my bag, and apologizing for the antiquity of his mother's Electric,[4] he led me in and we started home. We talked of the army, war, weather, his music, and the fellows whom he knows in the army. He showed me many places of interest as we passed them, especially the Catholic Cathedral. Finally, we drove between two stone pillars upon which were the words, "Cabanne Place."

My heart almost stopped beating. The Electric slowed up and with a wide swing we entered a driveway. On the side porch of a house a little way off I saw three people: Mrs. Walsh, Grace, and Sis. That picture leaped from some recess of my mind. Where had I seen it before? Or had I dreamt it?

Mrs. Walsh waived at me. We put the Electric away and went up to the porch. I shook hands with Mrs. Walsh, Grace, and Sis. From then on I moved as one in a dream. Rob immediately took me upstairs to my room, a large, elegant place.

Sis is tall for a girl, nearly as tall as I. She is not robust, not thin. Probably she would rightly be called slender. She is comely with golden hair, blue eyes, fair skin and a Grecian cast of countenance. She is fully grown up and when I saw her I found it hard to make myself believe that she was the sprite I had been in love with in South Haven. I am still trying to figure out whether it is she herself, or the memory of the little girl of five years ago I am in love with.

My memory of the sequence of events is a blur, so I will have to relate unconnected incidents as I remember them. I

---

4   The Detroit Electric was produced from 1907 until the Great Depression and marketed mainly to women and physicians. Both groups wanted a car that could start easily without having to hand-crank it, as was common practice at the time with gasoline-powered vehicles. Top speed was about twenty miles per hour, with a range of eighty miles (forty miles one way).

remember Sis taking me to the local library in her mother's Electric. On the way home I told Sis that the reason I had come to St. Louis was to say goodbye to her before I went to war.

She didn't say much.

We bumped between the posts leading into Cabanne Place. I told her I had never forgotten those two summers at South Haven. At this point, she said that she would write to me and knit me a sweater.

In the afternoon we went out to Florissant and I saw Ned Reynolds.[5] I had intended returning with Rob and taking the night train home, but Ned wouldn't hear of it. So, I stayed. As it grew dark we walked in the beautiful garden.

"How are you taking the war?" Ned asked.

"It's hard to say goodbye to my friends," I answered, "because I don't think I'm ever coming back."

I told him that my heart was breaking, as indeed it was. I sobbed in mortal agony. The floodgates of my pent-up grief were down and I told him everything, even my illusion about Sis. I don't believe that ever in my life was I in such mental agony as that night and the few days that preceded it. I bared my heart to Ned, my oldest friend, and I felt better after, and still do. But it was agony. He comforted me.

I spent three days at Florissant and met seventeen fellows from school that I knew. Ned and I had many interesting discussions on literature, economics and the war. I recovered my spirits and said goodbye to him Wednesday morning, Sept. 19th, about 11 o'clock. I drove into St. Louis with three fellows from the seminary. I could not help contrasting their state of mind and mine. If I hadn't met Sis, I might have made a good Jesuit.

I fear that psychologically I have been an odd fellow. I want

---

5   Cy's oldest friend, Ned Reynolds, left Woodlawn in 1916 to join the Jesuits at their novitiate in Florissant, Missouri. After the initial visit with the Walsh family, Rob drove Cy to see Ned.

very much to be like the rest of men, normal and congenial. My schoolfellows have, I imagine, looked askance at me. But I must not misrepresent. I believe that I have some few good friends, such as Ned and Toots. But to complete the irony, I believe that Sis looked on me as slightly odd.

This war, tho, ought to make me perfectly normal. I don't know whether there was any truth in the premonition or not. I go forth now, whether to death or not, God alone knows. I will try to die bravely, if it comes to that.

Just ten days later (Saturday, September 29th), I experienced one of the happiest moments of my life. Yes, I believe that it was the happiest. The joy was not the fierce, earthly kind. It was sort of a celestial rapture; -pure quintessential joy. I went to Confession, made a general confession of my past life. Father Lawrence told me that he was certain that I had never lost my baptismal innocence. The happiest moment of my life came after I came out of the confessional and realized it.

Then the war didn't matter. I had another of those convictions that I am going to be killed, but it seemed a blessing. For a while I saw things as they really are, and not as the world sees them. Death in the service of my country seemed a blessing. I have been uncertain, indecisive. Now I calmly see that it is right and necessary for me to go and do my bit to preserve the freedom of the world.

I applied for admission to the Aviation Corps. It is almost suicidal, but I am no longer going to be a dreamer. I will do my utmost and give my all.

Author's Note: Below is a more complete recollection of that day, as I remembered it nearly forty years later.

I was in downtown Chicago that day, over the noon hour, to find a particular book in Pawner's Bookstore. I met Paul Croarkin crossing Adams Street. It was by the sheerest chance. He had graduated several years previously from Saint Mary's,

Kansas, a Jesuit school, and was now trying to practice law with offices in an adjacent building. His parents and family lived in Woodlawn. We had known them a long time.

"What branch are you joining, Cy?"

"I was thinking of the Navy, the Mosquito fleet. I can get a job as a wireless operator."

"That's not for you. I have a much better spot for you—the Air Service!"

"You mean flying? Paul, I'm not up to that."

"How do you know? Let's go up to my office. I'll show you more about it."

In his office he produced a letter of recommendation and replies from big people in the Service. He had already been accepted and said he would help me get in. He had a blank application. I signed it then and there.

That night at supper I told the family. They were appalled. My sister started to whimper and my kid brother joined her.

"You'll be killed," they moaned.

Mother and Aunty looked scared. Finally, Mother said, "Now let your brother decide for himself. I'm sure he has looked into it carefully."

I assured them it was the very best branch. And that I was lucky to have such an influential friend.

What really prompted me to apply for admission to this most hazardous branch of the army? I have often asked myself that question, then and now.

Was it perhaps some memory of my grandfather who fought at the battle of Vicksburg and in several actions around New Orleans for the lost Confederate cause, and came home to die of wounds at age 36? Or of his cousin who had ridden with Jeb Stuart? Or of that young Irish Corbett who in another century had left Dublin University to join Napoleon, and who wound up a major general? Or, was it some genetic memory of the older and gallant Corbetts that prompted me?

No, frankly, it was not. It was simply that I wanted Sis Walsh to be proud of me. And that is the simple truth. I did it because of her. I felt I could not do otherwise.

THREE

The Farewell Parties Begin

LAST EVENING THERE WAS A PARTY HERE, a farewell party. Toots Weisenburger, a classmate and neighbor, had excitedly spread the word that I was going to the wars—but in the air! I was widely congratulated, too, by some of the teachers for being the first boy of old Ignatius to be accepted in the flying corps. My class and a few other fellows came to my house to celebrate. There were eighteen altogether: The fellows say that they are going to declare a holiday the day I go, and that the whole class is going to see me off. Several of them said that I had been elected class president.

The party left at 12:30. It was hard to say goodbye, but hope is what we live on. The party and everything seems far off and unreal. I cannot realize that I am going.

This morning Capt. Roberts called with Mrs. Wideman to reassure Mother that everything would be all right, which was a very gentlemanly thing for him to do. Mother and I went to high Mass together. Mother cried all thru mass. Fr. Hishen stopped us for a kind word on the way in. It is a blessing that things seem so unreal and dreamlike for me, or I don't see how I would go thru all this.

After dinner I went to St. Xavier's Convent and said

goodbye to Sister Benedicta.[6] We had a long talk. She feels very bad. After that we went up to Wideman's for supper. There were lots of people there. After supper John Ryan called for them to say goodbye to me. If we both get to France he is going to buy me the best dinner in Berlin; if not, I take him to the LaSalle.

After that there was a party at Dorothy Lyon's. Several people there. Had a good time. She promised to drive to Rockford some Sunday. (To visit me in training.)

October 1, 1917, Monday

Had a very dull day. Was exceedingly nervous now that all my work is done and that I have nothing to do. Didn't go to school.

No notice to report for duty. When it didn't come I went over to the board and was told that I am not going next Wednesday. When I am to go still seems to be a matter of conjecture. Leo McGivena says that the next 20% goes on Oct. 26th.

The climax of the day came at supper. I was ready "to jump out of my skin," so I took a walk and went to a picture show alone. Felt very lonely on the way home. When I got home Leo and Frank were here. We talked till 11 and then went for a walk. Stopped in a restaurant and had cakes and coffee. Walked around the Midway, up Greenwood Avenue, then they took the car. They certainly did me a lot of good. I like Leo (and Frank too) with all my heart. I can't say how much better I feel.

I have been much disturbed lately about losing out on my degree. I must have referred to it when I went to see Uncle Will recently. Anyway, he told me that when I came home from the War he would put me thru medicine or anything I wanted to study! I am much elated.

---

6   Sister Benedicta was born Nora Mary Corbett (1869–1936). She was Cy's aunt and the sister of Uncle Will Corbett.

This morning (Wednesday, Oct. 3rd) as I went into school Fr. Leahey told me told me that Fr. Furay, the rector, had returned from a conference, and that the news about my degree was unfavorable. I went to see the rector immediately but he was not there. I went a couple of times but could not find him in his room. I went to first class—Political Economy. (Fr. Lyons really has a big heart, and is interesting.)

Then I went to see the rector again. He told me that after much deliberation that I could get a degree only by going to school till Christmas. I told him that I was disappointed, -how I had thot and dreamed of this degree for the last four years. He advised me to apply to the Appeal Board for an extension. Then he told me to ask Fr. Leahey to figure up my credits.

I went to Leahey. The poor man was very busy but stopped everything to figure them up. We both were so excited that we added the whole business wrong.

I called up the Appeal Board to see about an extension, and after giving Fr. Furay the credits, I went downtown.

I interviewed the president of the University of Chicago, the great Mr. Judson. He was a very pleasant and courteous old man; a little short and stooped but very nice. He told me that his University had not as yet decided upon any course of action as regards to their students who were called to the army. He said it was likely that I could get an extension till Christmas.

I called up Mother and told her where I was and what I was doing and how disappointed I was about the degree. After I talked to her I went up to the 7th floor again to the Appeal Board proper. There they told me that my business was with the Local Board and gave me a note to the chairman of it.

I went to the Local Board. Just as I was getting off the Elevated I saw the men and a great crowd marching over 63rd Street. I was to have been with them, but at the last minute the government notified the local boards to send only 20% instead of 40%, as the barracks or something wasn't ready.

I went over to the station and saw them off at 1:30. Witnessed some pathetic sights, especially one of a brother and sister. She kept caressing him. It all but made me cry. I suppose they were all that was left of a family. I saw Mrs. Wideman, Mrs. Murphy, and met some of the boys who were going.

After it was all over I came home and had some dinner and went over to the Local Board. Mr. Eckland said that he was willing to give me an extension if I would get a statement of the case from the dean of our college. I said I would and started back to school.

On the way I stopped off at 47th St. to say goodbye to Grandma Corbett as per my promise to Sister Benedicta, who was there. I stayed three quarters of an hour and then went over to school.

I met Fr. Leahey as I was going in and he took me to his office. I told him of my adventures since I saw him earlier in the day. He started to write out the requested statement and I told him that I would much prefer having the rector give me a degree, or let me do some extra studying in some way so as to earn it, and let me go to war. He looked up and told me to go see the rector.

The rector told me—after I had told him about what had been done—that I should apply for an extension. If that didn't go thru he would then see about the degree. I told him that I would much prefer getting the degree in some way, and waive the extension. He looked up, and his face lit up, and he smiled and told me if that were the case that I would get the degree!

I was beside myself with Joy! I could hardly believe my ears. I went to Fr. Leahey and told him to tear up the note he had written as the rector was going to give me the degree. He grabbed me and hugged me hard and tight. He was happy, as if I had proved myself. I said that I guessed he had supposed that I was a slacker. He said that anyone who knew me would never even suspect that. I was so happy and overcome that I cried, and he hugged me some more. He tore up the note. He told me that he loved me and that I was the most honorable boy he had ever known.

I stayed with him and we smoked and talked of the army. I told him of my intuition that I was not coming back and he said that he didn't believe in intuitions. He said that he expected that I wouldn't be a private long and that in a few years I would come back a captain or something. Fond hopes! He said yes, that he thot my days of school were ended. I might adopt the army as a profession. He said later that life was a joke. I said yes, and the pity of it was that we all couldn't see the joke.

He walked to the door with me, called me a dear boy and told me again that he loved me. He asked me if I would do him a favor. I said yes, and without waiting to hear what it was (I sort of divined it) I kissed him and he me. And I kissed him again. He told me that I would always have his heart and his prayers, and I told him that he and old St. Ignatius would always have my heart and that tho I needed his prayers he didn't need mine. And with a final handshake I left him and both our eyes were wet.

This day has been more like the climax of a story than a reality.

October 16, 1917, Tuesday. Passed my Aviation physical exam!
Tonight I am very happy. I have the satisfaction of knowing that I am 100% man, for this day passed what is reputed to be the hardest physical test in the country, -the Aviation test. It lasted from 9 a.m. to 5 p.m.

Ed Colnon, Sherwin Murphy, and Leo McGivena all called up to find out if I passed it. My friends have not deserted me. A little while back, things looked dark with despair. I prayed for human consolation, if that was possible—and now I have found it. And happier of spirit, too. I am very happy. I got home from the physical just in time to meet at the Hayes Hotel and thence by automobile to the South Shore Country Club, probably the finest club in Chicago, where there was a banquet held in honor of the men who are going to Rockford.

It was very fine.

October 18, 1917, Thursday

Went to school today for a change. Attended French, Philosophy, History of Philosophy, and English classes. They all seemed very glad to see me. Everybody expresses, more or less tactlessly, surprise on my getting into the Aviation Corps.

October 26, 1917, Friday

Today I had dinner at Mrs. Reynolds's house (mother of friend Ned, who is at Florissant), with her and Lieutenant Doherty, her godson. He is in the Marines, the "Soldiers of the Sea," here on furlough from Virginia. (He is a graduate of the University of California.)

Paul Croarkin leaves tomorrow for Urbana and the Flying School. I had a long talk with him today. He is very hopeful as to the outcome of the war and his chances of surviving it.

Went to the Mission again tonight, and afterwards to confession. I feel very good tonight, -the deep dejection has left me. I have come to the conclusion that after all my high hopes, my ambitions, my eerie expectations—the eternal seeking after something, I know not what, is but the longing of the soul for eternity and heaven. They are inclinations of immortality. I was disappointed because I thot all were about to be snatched from me. Now I see that they are nearer than ever. There are but two things in life, -birth and death; and the fairer of these is death.

God has given me the grace to die happily, gallantly, and as a "gentleman unafraid." (If I should survive the war, I would not be surprised to find myself eventually down at Florissant.)

October 27, 1917, Saturday

This morning Paul Croarkin left for the Aviation School at Urbana, the University of Illinois. I saw him yesterday. He looked very fine in his $50 uniform.

October 30, 1917, Tuesday

Last night John Ryan, who is in Aviation also, came over. We practiced the telegraph code on a little line I have rigged up here, and we tried to converse in French. Yesterday noon Vincent Cunningham, Marc Ryan and myself took some copies of the Magazine over to Chicago Medical College (lately affiliated with Loyola University). On the way over we blew a tire. (It was Vincent's Mercer.)

Frank Kearns and Louise Jefferson were over Sunday night. I got Dorothy Lyons to come over and we had an informal party. Dorothy was really quite nice to me all evening. Just before we reached her home she said something that revealed to us all that she was under the impression that I was leaving the next day, Monday, for Urbana!

November 8, 1917, Thursday

A corporal from a recruiting office at 526 South State St. called me up today and told me to be ready to leave for the Aviation School at Urbana on Nov. 24.

So closely after the climax does the denouement follow that the reader must suspect this to be a work of fiction. My word of honor that it is not; that these events are true and are in exactly the order in which they are represented.

Tonight Marie and I went to Louise Jefferson's house in response to her invitation. Sherwin was there. I met her brother Ralph, who is in the fourth year of high school at St. Ignatius, and who has for a teacher Mr. Quinn, who is a close friend of Dan Lord's, who is, besides a bright star at St. Louis University, an old friend of Sherwin's. How our fates do intertwine!

November 9, 1917, Friday

I am now in the military service of the United States. I have been since about four o'clock this afternoon when I received the following notice when I reported at the recruiting station at 526 South State Street:

>War Department,
>The Adjutant General's Office
>Washington, November 5, 1917

From: The Adjutant General of the Army
To: Mr. Thomas C. Corbett
Subject: Induction into Service under the Selective Service Law

1. The Secretary of War directs that immediately upon the receipt by you of this letter you report, for induction as a selected man into the military service of the United States, to the Recruiting Officer, 526 South State Street, Chicago, Illinois.

2. When you report as directed in paragraph 1 of this letter, you will submit a copy of your registration certificate, copy of the notice to report to the local board for physical examination, and the enclosed three certified copies of this letter. You are in the military service of the United States from this date of the receipt by you of this letter and subject to orders from the officer to whom you are herein before directed to report. Compliance with these instructions relieves you from requirements for assembly by the local board.

(Signature illegible)
Adjutant General

From now on I am a soldier, till when, I wonder?

November 19, 1917, Monday

There are but three or four more entries that remain to be made in this diary. I leave either the 23rd or 24th. I was told both days by different men, so I don't know for sure. As the time approaches I feel much better. I am even gay. It is a sort of spiritual satisfaction of knowing that there is, if I may term it such, a star of destiny to guide my course. And God will be my guide.

Sherwin spoke of this diary last night, wondering what the entry would be like; and tonight also when he called up. He is interested in it. I am very glad. I also talked to Leo McGivena and Frank Kearns. There is a big farewell party for me tomorrow night at Leo's house.

I spent all day today working on my scrapbook. I mutilated all my old copies of the *Loyola University Magazine*, but it was worth it. There was an intangible satisfaction in seeing all the old work again. I think that I will get a great deal of pleasure from my scrapbook.

I had a phone call from an upperclassman at school. Lamb Hayes was studying law at nights and working days for the Steger Piano Company as a salesman. Charlie Byrne, advertising manager of the company, was only a name to me, but he was also an Ignatian, at least twelve years ahead. Lamb and Charlie wanted to know if I would permit them to use a poem of mine in an ad for pianos. There was no money in it, Lamb said, but it would undoubtedly promote my fortunes as a poet.

I said, "Sure." To tell Charlie that I was flattered. But which poem? He said it was "Music at Eve," a sonnet which had been published in the *Loyola University Magazine* during the year.

"Tell Charlie it's with my compliments."

"If you agreed, he said to tell you thanks. And that he'll return the favor someday."

(Later note: And he did return the favor. After the war, when men were scavenging for jobs, Steger's offered me a position as assistant to the president, which I accepted.)

November 20, 1917, Tuesday

All day I have felt an impulse to write in this diary, without knowing what I want to say.

This afternoon I took a long walk in the park and tried to contemplate my career and future state. I realize that this is the biggest change that has ever come into my life. From a life of quietude and inaction I am entering the most strenuous kind of work, with no end in view, and all uncertainty. But I have given the quiet life a trial and I have been more or less restless and melancholy now for action. It will be hard, very hard, and temptations await me. I tremble to think of them. I can do but what I am able—my best.

November 22, 1917, Thursday Evening

I did not write an account of the party (at Leo's house) two nights ago because it was 2 o'clock when I got home from seeing Norma Shulte home. Leo went with me, and we nearly had a falling-out on the way home arguing over a purely academic question.

The party was a fine affair. I appreciate deeply all that the folks are doing for me. We played "Bunco," ate, and danced. John Ryan said that he had the best time that he had had in a year. Sherwin just told me the same. Louise Jefferson told me quite frankly that she never expected to see me again. Everybody seemed to be a little "on edge." I suppose on account of the war and the likelihood of me leaving shortly.

Last Visit to St. Ignatius

Yesterday (Wednesday) I went over to school for the last time. We had Mass. I went in, in uniform, with the seniors. I was dazed all thru Mass. I knew it would be the last one I attended there as a student. I couldn't pray. Ed Colnon said later that he was distracted by my uniform and he said only four prayers. I said seven, I think.

After Mass was the quarterly distribution of scholastic

honors to the assembled high school and college, in the college hall. We seniors marched up thru the hall, behind the rector, to a place in the front row. This is the first time I have marched up thru the files of the attentive students. It makes me think of other years. How little I realized that, when that hour came to me, I would be marching as a soldier for the last time.

There was great clapping. The distribution proceeded thru the various classes, and at the end the rector gave a talk in which he spoke of the war and how many boys had gone to do their duty. He said, "And we have one with us today who is leaving shortly to fight for his country in the Aviation Corps." There was tremendous clapping and cheering. It lasted for about a half minute, I think—which, under the circumstances, is a long time. It was a proud moment.

After it was over the boys asked me how I liked the ovation they gave me. I was deeply touched. My friends among the students thought it a terrific adventure. The teachers, if they had any emotion, concealed it. They took it like the Jesuits took all the ups and downs of life, with studied indifference. Although one of them—Father Lyons, the burly, tough printer—called me aside and said, "Do me a favor, young squirt. Don't get yourself killed. You have too much future." (Flattering, but it did not speak well for his clairvoyance.)

I said goodbye to my friends, then I went and said goodbye to all the professors.

Fr. Leahey particularly was very good to me; he said that I knew that he would always be my friend, tho separated. Dear old Father Coppens, the ancient Belgian priest, stopped me in the hall, gave me a *Soldier's Prayer Book*, and his blessing. He was almost in tears. His little book became my lucky piece. I still have it.

About this time Father Furay, the rector of the college, issued a statement that all Seniors who joined the colors, and for that reason could not finish their last year, would be given their degree anyway. If Harvard could do it, he said, old Ignatius would do it, too. He was widely applauded.

Then downtown where I delivered a promised magazine to Lambert Hayes, and met Mr. Charles Byrnes, a famous alumnus from our place. Hayes told me about Dick Regan, one of our boys, in the British Flying Corps. Then I saw Frank Kearns and made a date to call later and go to supper with him. I walked across the Loop to says goodbye to Uncle Will, because I had promised to. But I wished I hadn't promised, because he isn't worth the effort. Little needs to be said.

Then I wandered around, half asleep, I believe. I didn't know where to go, and I was very tired. I stopped in the concert room at Lyon & Healy's but the concert was over just after I got there. I heard part of "Polonaise" from *Mignon*. At first I couldn't place it, but I know I had heard it at Rob's[7] house, on his Victrola. A curious lot of sensations swept over me.

I went from there down Michigan Avenue and stopped in the Art Institute, not so much in search of art as in search of a place where I could rest. I found a bench in the "Old Masters" room. And I sat there staring at a portrait (Dutch School, I believe) of a very thin, pale, ascetic-looking old lady. I fell asleep, I guess, until I heard footfalls. I wandered through the place, but it seemed insipid.

Then to Frank's office and to supper at the North American. Frank treated me to a fine dinner, but I could eat little more than the soup and ice cream. However, I got a strong cup of black coffee which braced me up.

I left during the dinner to phone Vincent, at Mother's suggestion. I was so tired and sick that I didn't see how I could go way over to his house that evening. From him I learned that there was no way of telling the class (whom Vinty had invited over in my honor) that it was off. So I said I'd go; but while

---

7 Rob Walsh, of St. Louis, brother of Cy's love interest, "Sis."

saying it I didn't see how I could. I guess we can always do a thing when we have to.

I said my last goodbye to my old friend Frank Kearns whom I had known over seven years. I met the class, or some of them—Ed, Cy, Si, Tom Walsh, Marc (Beckman came later)—on the station and we went out. Vincent met us at the train in his Mercer.

I Spend the Night at Vincent's

We had a jolly, a fine, convivial time, all evening. Annis had two friends there. Bunco, supper, dancing, playing on the piano.

Ed—"Si, is that Chopin Annis is playing?"

Si—"No, that's impromptu."

Gads, I hated to leave them, they are such fine, good-hearted fellows. The party broke up at 12 and I stayed all night with Vincent.

Up at 11:30 this morning. Breakfast, talked, played piano, said goodbye—and left the Cunninghams. They are all hoping for the best. Vincent and I talked long this morning. He is my friend and I am his friend forever; no matter what happens. I saw a good deal into his hopes and his life, and he into mine.

He took me to Sheridan Road Station, with snow and sleet. I told him not to forget me; he said he wouldn't. He said I was one of the few boys he had ever been intimate with. I said that I would never forget him. And so we parted. I will see him again when I leave.

Stopped on the way home and got an army overcoat and a service suit at one of the stores.

Yesterday I had a long talk with Fr. Lomasney. I asked him if in all his study he had run across a cure for melancholy. He said no, but suggested friends, books, diversions. I said that once I thot that the panacea was philosophy. He shook his head.

He gave me some beautiful hand-painted scapulars, one

pair of which I gave to Annis. (Tho they were a gift, they were too nice for me.) The other pair is for my Mother, and I have a plain pair and a holy picture left. They are beside me as I write this.

In return for the gift (of the scapulars), Annis told me something that she said to someone the evening before. She said that I looked like Sir Galahad, which I consider to be the handsomest compliment that I have ever received.

I am restive and nervous tonight, as the end approaches. What can I say now? There is much to say and to finish saying but I am in no condition to say it.

Friends, friends—

November 23, 1917, Friday Evening
The End
Now the time of my departure approaches. This is the last time I will make an entry in this diary. Though thru the eye of God I hope to return from this war, I will not keep another diary, so now the end.

There was much to be said but it escapes me now. I leave that to the man who will write my memoirs, if that ever happens. I would like to have Mr. Richard Murphy (the father of Sherwin) and Father Lomasney decide upon the worth of this book and upon the one to write my memoir. Fr. Lomasney may be found at St. Ignatius, and Mr. Murphy at 4821 Dorchester Ave., Chicago, Ill.

I took another physical examination today and barely passed it. I was so underweight. I have said goodbye to everybody. Mother and the family have had a good many tears with me. And now naught remains but to go.

So goodbye. I thank my Mother for her years of loving care. I can never hope to be able to repay them in one hundredth part. I thank my dead Father for years of labor. I thank my Aunt for all she has done for me since I was a child, and I thank my brother and sister for the years of love and friendship. I ask pardon of all my enemies; and for all harsh things I may have said within this diary. Of my friends, I ask of them love and that they shall not forget me.

Mother, Mother, dearest and sublimest of women, goodbye. You are nearer to God so pray for me that all may come out alright. Aunt, brother and sister, goodbye. I love you all and especially you, my mother, with a love I cannot fathom.

And now the end—
"The rest is silence."

~1970 Recollection:

November 24, 1917. I still see the scene as if it were yesterday. At the Illinois Central Railroad's 63rd Street station. Mother, Aunty, my young sister and brother lined up in a company front, so to speak, sadly waving goodbye and looking very dubious about my future. Two others were there. Mrs. Lyons, motherly, very Irish, and her lovely, blue-eyed daughter, Dorothy (my one-time girlfriend). All of them acted as though they would never see me again but were bound to put a good face on it. Mother seemed bewildered, Aunty stoic, Mrs. Lyons weepy, her daughter uncomfortable. I kissed them all, boarded the coach, the train jerked into motion and I was off to the wars. That scene will never die.

Cy Corbett boards the train for the Army Air Corps
(Courtesy of T.C. Corbett Family Archives)

PART TWO:

I Am Summoned to the War

Cadet T.C. Corbett

FOUR

Ground School

GROUND SCHOOL AT THE UNIVERSITY OF ILLINOIS! It was a huge place with buildings everywhere, in contrast to old St. Ignatius College, which had only one. The hordes of students seemed somehow different. And it was strange to see a few girls on the campus. I was in a whole new world.

We were housed in a handsome building not yet quite finished, the women's dorm, four cadets to a tiny room. We marched in formation to various classes, always in different buildings. We studied such subjects as Machine Guns, Aerial Navigation, Army Regulations, a smattering of Astronomy, the Morse Code (Wireless Telegraphy), the theory of Flight and Military Tactics. To most of those vigorous young Americans the curriculum seemed highly irrelevant to fighting a war and unseating Kaiser Wilhelm.

Our instructors were bright young graduate students and associate professors in ill-fitting regulation uniforms propounding subjects not familiar to them. It embarrassed some, made others belligerent. The whole thing seemed ridiculous. We decided that Ground School was simply a time-killing device to keep the men busy while the government caught up on the manufacture of airplanes. It struck us as a war of fumbling amateurs.

But there was one real soldier-figure among us—a wizened-up grumpy little guy whose battered campaign hat and rag-tag uniform bespoke countless years of army pay and army red tape: the company bugler. And that was all he did. Said to be an expert goldbricker and a last survivor of the Philippines campaigns, he was not much of a musician. Or, was he? There was always one awfully sour note somewhere in his renditions. That was his trademark, his personal protest against the large inequities of life. But when he was working well, and on key, you could almost see the soldiers of another war scrambling to their places in a company front.

* * *

~1970 Recollection:

Cudgeling my brains, at this late date, to recall those scenes and people, I can recall an irrelevant but humorous incident. The bugle sounded at 5 a.m. And we were routed out of our uncomfortable but warm army cots to line up as a company in the front of the building. After the roll call, and reading of orders of the day, we spaced out to do the calisthenics, this day, in deep snow.

Some of the men would catch an extra five minutes of sleep by neglecting to get dressed. They would put on shoes and puttees, and the long army overcoat would conceal their pajamas. The sergeant in charge must have gotten wind of it, or perhaps it was just a routine thing that every squadron tried once. Anyway, this particular morning he ordered, "Overcoats off!" The men folded them carefully and laid them in snow and went thru the exercises freezing in their pajamas. The tough sergeant, veteran of 35 years, called out the numbers to the end, precisely as he did every morning, never cracking a smile, and pretending not to notice a thing.

The men I can remember? Paul Croarkin I saw in Ground School once or twice. He was four weeks ahead of me. He became a class pilot, survived in the war and lived out his life in Washington, D.C., where he was a governmental lawyer.

Of my three roommates, Harwood White, the brother of the writer Stewart Edward White, had been in his last year at Princeton, and a very bright lad he was, indeed. I never saw him crack a book but he always got the top mark in his class or near it. He was coldly intellectual and a little hostile to us groundlings, but I thot his able brain would carry him far in life. He spent it at a fancy tennis club in California, as a tennis coach and instructor of champions. He was from Lansing, Michigan, where his father had been an eminent judge.

His pal and buddy, Roy Fitzgerald, another roommate and from Princeton, also was his opposite—warm, vigorous, and outspoken and Irish. He was from Grand Rapids. Both were very conscious of the social position they felt a top Ivy League education gave them. The fourth roommate, a lanky Westerner by the name of Kern, and I were just the proletarian element. And made a little uncomfortable in our own role.

The worst bête noire of the course was the Code. You had to be able to send and receive 12 words a minute and many of the men nearly lost their minds trying to master it. It is said that to some persons it is psychologically impossible to hear words in the Code, but that was not known then. Many flunked out unnecessarily.

Armchair generals had imagined that all pilots should be adept in Code, the only means then of communicating with the ground. The main purpose was for artillery "spotting"—to wire back whether a burst was over or short. But as it turned out, the Artillery developed their own expert observers who had to be trained in more things than Code.

All in all, even if you survived it, Ground School was a big bore, and we were very glad, at the end of eight weeks, to be given a small certificate, three days leave, and sent to Texas.

~1970 Recollection

To Camp Dick

The army sent us south in railroad equipment it must have gotten out of a museum. The coaches were said to be from 1880, and the engine was only a few years newer. It took us seven days to get from Champaign, Illinois, to Dallas, Texas. The train seemed to wander all over Iowa and Missouri, stopping frequently for repairs. We even stopped at crossroad restaurants for meals, for there was no diner or supply car hitched to our train.

The men were bored to extinction. Someone started a craps game which kept going day and night until one man had all the money on the train—$2,500, in cash. His name was Covington, and he was from Covington, Kentucky. Everyone said he was a phenomenally lucky player. Years later he and a partner owned a small advertising agency in New York City. On rainy days, it was said, they stayed inside and shot craps for the agency. I met him once. He was just a pleasant Southern boy that no one would suspect to be such a demon with the dice. But no one else of his era was so widely remembered.

We finally arrived, not at a flying field, but at Camp Dick in the heart of Dallas. It was really the Dallas County Fairgrounds remade into a camp; an army reservoir, a place to keep the men until the flying fields could accept them. The actual airfields were behind on training because they lacked ships and instructors.

Camp Dick was located a few miles from the business district of Dallas and occupied several square blocks, consisting of various exhibition buildings built around a one-mile race track. Like the lotus flowers, the Fairgrounds blossom forth with the Fair for a few short weeks each year and then sink back into oblivion.

For the war effort, they cleaned out the old horse and cattle barns, and we lived in them. Occasional inch-wide spaces between the boards in the walls let in the cold Texas night air. Washing facilities consisted of tin basins on a long bench outside the building with two or three faucets. Often we had to break the ice on a cold morning. I can't remember any heat in the place. We were much up against the elements when a dreaded Texas Norther blew.

We were the second squadron in. An outfit from Austin, Texas, beat us by a half hour. After depositing luggage on the assigned bunks the men gathered sadly, silently in a little group, once they realized the extent of the disaster. Ground School had been bad enough, but this! I remember wondering, "Why does this country always treat its soldiers so badly?" The gloom was profound. It was probably a low point in the army experience for most of us.

We hardened up and soon Camp Dick was not so bad. I never found out who the Dick was it was named after, but at best it was a doubtful honor. The men were young, vigorous and cheerful. And could take anything so they reacted splendidly. I have always marveled at the resiliency of the Yankee male.

Rack my brain as I will, I can't remember anything of a remarkable nature happening at Camp Dick, except that once or twice a hopeless cadet made a forced landing by our parade grounds. We did little more than drill during our six weeks there. We drilled on the streets, which were wide and winding, and on the parade ground until we were heartily sick of the *Manual of Arms*. It was an asinine waste of energy for future pilots. No doubt some antedated general of the Kipling tradition had decreed it because he couldn't think of anything that might be pertinent to the new branch.

Camp Dick, like Ground School, was mostly a drag, and I can't think now of anything good to say about it. We got too much physical exercise and were always tired. We learned nothing. We made no new friends. We were officered by bland civilian 90-day wonders, who largely didn't know what they were about. We were lectured to, a couple of times, for the sake of morale, by flyers returned from the front whose stuff was so unclear and unenlightening that we judged they must have been drunk most of the time.

We were very glad when, at the end of this six-week trip of military purgatory, army trucks came for us and our lockers, and delivered us to Love Field, eight miles out of Dallas, where we would at least be near airplanes.

***

1923 Pilgrimage: Camp Dick

Years later, when I arrived in Dallas on my Pilgrimage, the Fair was just over, and the Fairgrounds had beaten its annual retreat to the nethermost part of the Dallas public mind. The people I talked to seemed to have difficulty in remembering it as Camp Dick at all. But to the thousands of boys who passed through this reservoir camp on their way to the flying fields, it will never be anything other than old Camp Dick, with its cow sheds and horse barns and pigsties hastily pressed into service for human quarters.

As I walked down the main street towards the horse barns where Squadron #2 from the University of Illinois was first quartered, there came to memory the first time we came down that street, a long column of platoons, marching to the thunder of drums in perfect unison. And then the fifes and the deep voiced horns broke into the blood-stirring magic of Sousa's "America Forever."[8] I can still remember the thrill down my back then to think that this is my land, and these fine men are my brothers. War has its high spots as well as its deep miseries.

---

8 TCC refers to Sousa's "Stars and Stripes Forever" as it was sometimes called by the cadets at the time.

I found that old, one-story wooden shack called the Agricultural Building where we were quartered, and went around to the rear, but the old sliding door was nailed shut. The yard in front of it, where we used to "fall out and fall in," was still deep in that which five years never changes—the Texas mud.

Finding a door that was open, I went inside and stood on the spot where my bunk had been—where, dead tired and heartsick, I had written home a long letter about Love Field after seeing it for the first time while there on guard duty. As I wrote, that night, Frank Chance was playing on his fiddle "Mighty Lak' A Rose," and a pathos clutched my soul—a great longing for home and love and laughter that seemed to have fled forever. That, of the whole war, was my most poignant hour.

The inside of the old barracks had been cut up into booths at the recent Fair, and an ancient Negro was sweeping out the debris. Despite its altered appearance it was not hard to see the orderly bunks row on row, with lockers at the ends, and the boys gathered around the one inverted-funnel stove during our first experience of a "Texas Norther."

Last, I hired a horse and cantered around the old race track where we had done "squads east and squads west" interminably with rifles that got heavier each hour, where our ranks had "deployed for skirmish," where our wide platoons would "pass in review." On this same field Vernon Castle[9] had put down a Curtiss Canuck one day in the prettiest of landings. But they were gone, all gone, messieurs, those fine boys, those old days—the glory both departed.

---

9   Vernon Castle and his wife, Irene, were a husband-and-wife dancing team who appeared in silent films and on Broadway during the early twentieth century. They were credited with popularizing the foxtrot. His actual name was William Vernon Blyth, born in Norwich, England. He enlisted in the Royal Flying Corps, completing three hundred missions over the Western Front, shooting down two planes. He was assigned to Canada to train new pilots, then transferred to Camp Taliaferro.

Cadet T.C. Corbett

Editor's Note: Cy Corbett was stationed at Camp Dick from February 6 until March 1, 1918, when he was transferred to Love Field. Men from Camp Dick were often assigned guard duty at Love Field, which allowed them to observe life at the field and learn what to expect when they actually began their flight training at Love. As mentioned below in Cy's narrative, he wrote a letter home to one of his best friends, Sherwin Murphy, describing guard duty there.

Here is an old letter dated January 18, 1918, written when Love Field was the biggest place in Texas. I was still stationed at Camp Dick, but looked forward to my eventual transfer to the place where cadets earned their wings.

Dear Sherwin:

Twenty-four men from our squadron, among whom was your humble servant, were on guard at Love Field from noon Sunday until Monday noon. When we marched into our barracks Monday, wet, tired, stiff, sleepless and muddy, we knew to some extent how the doughboys must feel when they leave the trenches. Have you ever been dog-tired? That is, hungry, sore in every muscle—your joints seem to work like rusty hinges as you walk—ambitionless, apathetic, and dazed from loss of sleep. That's what dog-tired means. And that's what I was Monday afternoon.

I went to bed and slept until they woke me up for mess. After mess I turned in again and slept all night. So tonight, after a good meal in town, I feel far more able to write a letter. I will try to tell you something about my experience on guard.

We left here (Camp Dick) last Sunday morning and arrived at Love Field at noon. I went on guard immediately and stayed on till 2:30. Nothing eventful happened except that I saw a plane wheeled out of the hangars. She was cranked up, and taxied across the field. The moment her wheels left the ground it was a sensation to me, trudging along with a gun on my shoulder. I watched the plane rise, circle around the field and come back. The flyer's path of flight was directly above the point where I was standing. I knew he could see me for he was only about eight hundred feet up. As he passed over I halted, and brought my rifle to "present arms," which is the salute accorded only to an officer by a guard. He must have been surprised, for he banked sharply and came back, cut a circle, and was off again.

That was the only remarkable thing that happened on that relief. I saluted innumerable officers and my shoulder got very stiff. After being relieved we had dinner and "rode the springs" which means that we unrolled our two blankets and tried to camouflage the sharp springs on an unmattressed bed. Awoke at six and went on guard again.

While I was pacing my post a big automobile drove past me,

and I presented arms. A Canadian airman was driving. He returned my salute and stopped a little way down the road. An elderly lady, whom one would judge to be his mother, got out, and also two girls. They all walked across the field to a plane that was waiting to be rolled into the hangar for the night. They examined it and the officer seemed to be explaining the various parts to them. The girls climbed into the cockpit and worked the controls. Presently they returned to the waiting car and drove past me again. I came to present arms, he saluted again, and they drove down the road and out of sight. It was Vernon Castle!

I was on again from 12–2 a.m. It was a dreary time and I tramped around half asleep. I had an encounter with the officer of the day, and was all but run over by a Ford which insisted on taking the wrong road, and marched a man without a pass to the guardhouse.

The morning, from six to eight, was a wonderful time. The first thing I remember (I was half asleep myself), was hearing somebody down the road whistling "The End of a Perfect Day." It was heartbreaking coming out of the darkness. The man who whistled it must have been a good deal of an artist, and yet in a way it was so incongruous that I didn't know whether to sob or laugh. Soon things began to liven up. The hangars lighted up one by one. Men were moving along the road. First mechanics, and then cadets intermixed with officers. And leather-coated figures that were either cadets or officers, I don't know which, but I do know that they were flyers.

Motorcycles were whizzing by at forty miles an hour, squawking raucously. Automobiles went by, ambulances, too; supply trucks and every sort of thing that runs on wheels. It was plain pandemonium for a while. One hangar opened wide its great doors and a plane was pushed out, propelled by a half-dozen men. All down the road planes were coming out, and, propelled by a squad of mechanics, they crossed the dusty highway and rested in the field. A company of leather-coated figures marched past me at "double time."

I saw a mechanic twisting a propeller. He twisted it a half dozen turns, then stepped back. After a brief pause, he stepped up again to the shining blade. A quick jerk, and the thing kicked around a few times, and finally started whirling with a deep drone. The machine taxied out onto the field, gaining speed. Its tail lifted off the ground first, and next its wheels, a little unsteadily. It touched again and then shot up. Several other planes repeated this process until I could count at least sixteen of them in the air at one time.

I stood, fascinated. Finally relief came and we had some breakfast. The guard was over. After a bit, our truck arrived. We climbed in and we went down the road, out of the gate and along the country road that runs from Love Field to Dallas, several planes following us, swooping overhead. The flyers waved a goodbye, and we left behind us an equally fascinating and impossible place—a flying field.

Don't forget to write soon, and tell me all the news from home.

Sincerely yours,
Cyril

Less than a month after my initial letter to Sherwin, I wrote home again:

Vernon Castle Dies Feb. 15, 1918

I suppose you folks were all surprised by the news of Vernon Castle's death.[10] He was an instructor at one of the flying fields in Fort Worth. He was a clever flyer, and well liked by the men. He was a rather tall, slim man with ruddy hair. I was fortunate

---

10 As noted later in the text, Castle attempted to take evasive action to avoid collision with another plane. It was said that, other than Vernon's death, "Neither the other pilot, his student cadet, or Vernon's pet monkey, Jeffrey, were seriously injured."

in being able to see him at close range last Saturday at The Dansant[11] given in his honor at the Adolphus Hotel. He had a broad English accent; his uniform and Sam Brown belt were resplendent to the nth degree. He didn't dance very much but sat at a table talking to friends.

Vernon Castle with his pet monkey, Jeffrey, taken in January 1918
(Courtesy of Bain Collection, Library of Congress)

---

11 A dance held while afternoon tea is served, popular in the 1920s and 1930s.

This afternoon a Curtiss machine landed in our drill field. There were two men in the plane, a Canadian commissioned instructor and a cadet in the R.F.C. I had a talk with the cadet while his instructor was gone. He said that Castle's death, even, was an example of his high sportsmanship. In an effort to avoid a collision which he was about to land, he attempted an Immelmann[12] close to the ground, hoping to be able to come out of it before he hit. But the feat was impossible. He was killed saving another man's life. That happened only this morning.

I cannot get Vernon Castle out of my mind tonight.

---

12 An Immelmann is a dangerous aerobatic maneuver whereby the pilot performs a half loop followed by a half roll, thus reversing direction and increasing height.

FIVE

1923 Pilgrimage

KIPLING SAYS THAT THE DEFINITION OF A SOLDIER is a man who always wants to be somewhere else. Perhaps it was a hangover from my soldiering days, but for five years I had wanted to be back in Dallas, back at Love Field where I had first learned that it was possible to restrain, with varying success, the law of gravitation.

I knew that the field was in ruins, that the captains and the cadets had departed, and that no more were there ships roaring on the line before dawn where only the cherry red of their exhaust pipes could be seen. These were gone, I knew, and the busy scene of the flying field had been dissolved forever, but nevertheless, I wanted to go back.

And back I went one year in the fall, when the glory of the semitropical summer was waning in Dallas. There was no intention of writing this account. I wanted only to stand once more on that memorable ground, and to feel the magic of those departed days.

And so, on one October afternoon in 1923, I found myself in that great refuge of all homeless Americans—the hotel, sitting in a high-backed Tudor chair in the lobby and listening to a young chap playing a grand piano. Played it, I said, but I should have said that he was meditating on it and its mellow and lyric notes came to me as the voice of a poet intoning the cantos of some epic story.

And I tried to think how this scene was so different from the Dallas of five years ago, populated, as it was then, by slim, straight boys in uniform with boots and bars and wings. The wings were what you saw—always. And these boys were gone, all gone, and so the old Adolphus Hotel, too, seemed different. As I sat there listening to the chap playing, again I could see those slim wraiths, singly and in small groups, happy, laughing, eager, troop through there on the way to dinner or to dance through their brief holiday. I still could hear their boot heels clicking on the steps. I saw their wings and bright uniforms— those lean, courageous figures. But they are gone utterly, completely, from this place that knew their footfalls and here was I, a lonely wanderer, drawn curiously back in pilgrimage.

He touched the ancient chords, evoking the ineffable, eternal sadness that is Life. The sweet and bitter melody mounted in its flight, awaking in the heart the conviction that here, at last, is the meaning and the unity that runs through all things: that the spectacle of life is beautiful, that the actions of men, their tears, their sacrifices and their high courage rises as a visual melody.

Then it was, while listening to that stringed reverie, that I determined to set down what I could of the old memories, to set them down truthfully, including both the pleasant and the bitter; for I am not one of your saccharinists who believes that an attractive story must be sugarcoated. There is no thing more beautiful than reality.

More difficult than the pursuit of butterflies is the pursuit of ghosts—ghosts of days that are dead and past, of men who have departed the scene, of jests and ribaldries that time has cut short in their laughter. What could I do except to visit these scenes; what was there but to go over a few ragged letters that had survived? And I talked with three old fliers, and over our cigars and coffee we tried to remember.

From these poor properties, and from that witchery of the mind that remembers things long forgotten when one steps on their familiar ground, I have tried, here, to conjure up a few scenes from the feverish days of 1917 and 1918.

Love Field Open House "Flyin' Frolic," Nov. 12–13, 1918.
(Courtesy of National Archives)

Sergeant Williams Calls the Roll

Prowling, yesterday, around the shabby hangars and through ruined barracks, I could feel the magic of long-forgotten days, could reconstruct the scene from these shabby properties.

I sat on the steps of barracks #2 and it was again the star-studded darkness of an early Texas morning. We were again doing calisthenics to the rhythm of a voice calling out the numbers in darkness. A faint cool breeze was stirring as I watched the Morning Star, remembering that it looked down on loved ones far away. Sleepily, I considered the mystic thing we call life. Then would always come to me the verbal music of Euripides, "Dark indeed was it, with only the Morning Star."

From out on the line came the rhythmic put-put-put of a cold engine warming up, invisible in the darkness except the cherry red of its exhaust flame. From all up and down the line came the steady drone of ships warming up. Unseen motorcycles roared past and were gone.

Out on the invisible field a motor opened wide and across the dark, between the hangars streaked the small red flame of its exhaust as the pilot traversed the field in darkness to rise and greet the dawn. The chromatic rhythm of motors up and down the line sounded many notes that mingled in symphonic chords.

The Morning Star faded out and the sky grew gray. Hurrying figures in leather coats or monkey suits with the chin straps of their helmets dangling, milled around among the planes and the slow spectre of the "Meat Wagon" moving to its post of vigil. And then the full dawn broke on gleaming wings, rushing across the field to take the air. This, my brothers, was the poetry, the adventures, the strong wine of our flying days.

A line of "Meat Wagons" at the ready in front of the hospital building at Love Field, Texas, taken Aug. 8, 1918.
(Courtesy of National Archives)

The scene changes. It is just before Retreat and the sun is sinking behind the Maple Avenue road. The cadets are at attention, lined up in two long columns to answer Roll Call. The lean familiar figure of Sergeant Williams is calling off the names. He is trying to be hardboiled, and on his lips is a slightly sardonic smile, as he rattles off the names. The men answer, "Year," "Present," "Yo," and some humorist, "Yo Ho." "Whizzat-man," calls Williams, and he goes right on down the list with never a stop until some cadet fails to answer. Then, "Answer yore name, men," and comes the belated "here." Sarge was a good fellow.

Where are they now?—these old familiar names—Franceen, Lutz, Hodgkin, Stoll, Glasscock, Midkuff, Wenban. And where are you, Mugglestone, Razor, Kraus, Faneuf, Frick, De Learie, Dolphan, Finsterwald, and Frogg? The answer "here" comes from the four corners of the earth, and from the world beyond. And I get up sadly from the steps of the old barracks, for no magic of imagination can bring them back—these brave boys, whose memory is as fragrant as an "Air" from Chopin.

Love Field

I made a trip out to old Love Field this morning. The field is one and one-fourth miles square, and is located six miles from town, between two parallel roads, Maple and Lemon Avenues. I hired a Ford and a young fellow to drive it. This chap had been a roustabout and a rigger at Burkeburnett,[13] and he could do everything with a Ford but loop it. We went out through a section of Dallas which was composed mostly of humble cottages, passing here and there through the more ambitious bungalow sections. We passed old Dallas University, always a good landmark from the air.

Out still farther where the houses become more humble were, here and there, the rack and ruin of what were known as

---

13 In 1918 an oil boom began in Burkeburnett, Texas.

chicken dinner farms. These were popular five years ago but they have fallen into disuse.

Our first sight of Love Field was the old Machine Repair Depot called the "A.R.D." (Air Repair Depot). Its old barracks and machine shops have been repainted and repaired and sold for dwellings to civilian workmen. Where the old A.R.D. stood are three large industrial buildings, a chemical factory, a pump works and a machine shop. The old Airdrome is overgrown with weeds and clumps of alfalfa and wild cotton, in great contrast to the old landing terrace, which was as smooth as a golf green. The old wire fences are down in spots, but from a distance the great hangars appear intact.

As we pulled up to the Maple Avenue entrance to the field, we passed a long red brick building, a cotton factory. Surrounding it in every direction were rows of cheap wooden cottages just completed for the factory workmen. There was also a general store and the "Love Field Hotel," a small wooden structure.

Then we came opposite the line of hangars. No paint for five years, windows shattered, great sliding doors broken down or left standing open, revealing the emptiness within. The road itself was worn to bad repair. On the left the first row of barracks, occupied in the old days by enlisted mechanics, was gone completely, and in its stead a few charred sticks and sooty bricks. A line of washstands, blackened with mold, alone, stood out. The neat gravel paths and the green yard in front of the Headquarters building were gone, and the building itself paintless, windows broken, suggested that authority itself cannot resist decay. The cadet barracks, mess halls and officers club were in the same state of decay.

How the great and the lowly have fallen! Alike in ruin were the Officers' Mess and the barracks where the grounded Dodos stayed. Windows were out and doors barred shut, and the wooden sidewalks had rotted away. Weeds and the wild grass of this country were trying to cover the ruins, and a cow grazed contentedly beside the once resplendent Officers' Club.

And on the top of Hangar 6 old "Annie Mometer" was gone and the old white sock, flying in the wind to show its direction, was no more. I climbed the superstructure of Hangar 6 to the lookout tower and the prospects of empty hangars, barracks in ruin, and the headquarters building falling apart was dismal indeed to one who had seen them all buzzing with wartime activity. A herd of cattle grazed on the landing field. Even the old water tower had a forsaken look.

But on the Airdrome beyond the hangars and its flanking roads were a line of powerful D.H.'s—eight of them in all—with one small S.E.5 and a Martin Bomber. A dozen officers in leather coats and mechanics in "monkey suits" with interested spectators completed the picture. They were the 26th Aero Squadron flown down from Kelly to put on the Air Carnival Sunday. Among them was one boy I trained with—Lieutenant Gates—who had been in the service ever since. There was one Major, four Captains, and the rest First Lieutenants and a young Boston Bull pup, a mascot.

The de Havillands were observation ships; the rear cockpit of each had a Browning Gun on swivel. On the body of the plane or the fuselage was a shield of gold with a fist of blue upon it—the insignium of the squadron. These great ships with their tilted-up wings, in marked dihedral, are curiously like eagles at rest. They form the backbone of the country's air force. The little S.E.5, standing like a hawk among eagles, was the Major's ship—the flagship of the squadron. A corps of mechanics were tuning up the bombers' engines, and in the distance a Curtiss was roaring wide open.

Among the men there was a disparity of uniform that you may find in no other branch. The Major, a husky smiling fellow, was resplendent in the very latest of Sam Brown belts with khaki tunic and cream-colored whipcord pants. This combination is thought to be very swank. He had the crushed military cap of the English. The other men were arrayed variously from the complete uniform to the complete monkey suit with goggles and a skull helmet for headdress. They were waiting impatiently for two lagging members of the squadron to arrive. I left them after exchanging addresses with Gates.

Driving back we caught a fleeting glimpse of Bockman's Dam, where Cadet Richmond, on fire, landed in the only tree on the field, and by the spot where Major Netherwood crashed as I stood talking to a sentry. Most of the buildings were now gone and the elements want only a year or two more to complete this work of ruin.

Armistice Day

As we stood there beside my old friend de Gozzaldi's little roadster watching a dozen planes cavorting around in the blue, I was entirely at a loss for something to which to compare the courage of these men who have made all space above the treetops their playground.

If ever there was courage in humans it is here. I know not what to liken them to. Certainly not to their ancestors who fought with lance and broadsword, not to men who fought in galley and great sailing vessel, not to those who in our own time fought in trench and dugout. For what is the courage of these compared to 2,000-foot vertical zooms from the ground to 200 feet with a neat barrel roll at top (called a chandelle). There were Immelmans, Falling Leaves, and half loops that would turn into a roll or "wing over." These little scouts and Voights did what no bird ever attempted, and, what one must think, God never intended to be done in the air.

These wonderful maneuvers, which appear so simple, are but the net result of many component forces which the skilled judgment of the flyer mixes in proper proportion to obtain the result. Remember, that even a simple loop is the result of such component forces as centrifugal and centripetal forces, gravity, forward torque of the plane, momentum and air resistance. And in the pilot's brain, sense of balance and sense of motion forward, is centered the control of all these forces.

But the most marvelous thing is that the nerve center, the ganglia of these great birds, are men who until two short decades ago were entirely ground animals, whose ancestors for countless centuries tramped the earth and fought with mace and sword, axe and arch and arrow; whose ancestors fought a running fight with beasts of earth that were stronger and fiercer than they. And these flyers themselves are but children of men who hunger and sleep and whose passions burn for a little before they die.

Watching them, one gradually begins to feel the third dimension. Hearing the drone of the motor and the screech of wind in the wires of a plane passing close, comes a sense of the flatness of earth and how abbreviated is man and all his works and days.

A small stone obelisk, inscribed with a tablet in bronze to "Lieut. John Love, Officer of the 1st Virginia Cavalry,"[14] stands at the eastern entrance to the field. The stone is grown around with weeds and the clayish mud of Texas. On it are tablets to Parker Bruce and William Insinger, both of whom I saw die. There are the names of many other gallant boys whom I did not know or could not remember.

In far-off Greece on the plains of Marathon, there is another grave of soldiers, old and out of mind, when the race from which these boys sprung was still unforgotten. It bears the inscription—

"Stranger, tell the Spartan hosts that here we lie,
faithful to their trusts and bidding."

***

---

14 Multiple sources say the field was named after Moss L. Love, who, while assigned to the US Army 11th Cavalry, died in an airplane crash near San Diego, California, on September 4, 1913, becoming the tenth fatality in U.S. Army aviation history. Love Field was named by the United States Army on October 19, 1917. It is possible the creator of the stone accidentally commemorated John Love, who did fight in the Virginia Calvary.

As I boarded the train home after my brief respite from the writing of ads, it was with the deep conviction that there was never a journey back, and no returning. For it is a part of the pathos of distance that what is past is gone forever.

SIX

Pilot Training

Altho our group from the University of Illinois was the second squadron to occupy the newly organized Camp Dick, we were latecomers at Love Field. A couple of men brought my army locker in and plopped it down at the foot of an unoccupied cot. Bud Fisher, the man on the adjoining cot, arose and introduced himself. He had been here a couple of weeks but had not had a chance to fly yet. Everything was slow. There was a great dearth of planes. The dumb cadets cracked up too many. However, he had made several contacts in town. He would introduce me around next weekend. No need whatsoever to be homesick. He talked a mile a minute.

My neighbor on the other side, a tall, dark, young fellow, was sprawled on his cot, reading a scientific journal and looking annoyed. Further down the line a group of five or six were singing college songs in close harmony. Men were coming and going to the washroom with shaving things, towels over their shoulders. It was the usual barracks scene when the men have a little time to themselves. But there was something distressing about it. I was already a little homesick.

Bud was as good as his word. We went to town together every weekend and I gradually got to meet all his friends: Peg Thornton and her suitor Marshall Mulvahill, the Merrills, the young widow McLaughlan, Audry and Millicent, beautiful eighteen-year-old twins whose father owned a big restaurant in downtown Dallas, another family who owned a cotton-gin business, and several other people. How he managed to meet so many of Dallas's upper crust in so short a time is anybody's guess. We were seldom at a loss for a place to eat supper Saturday night, or dinner Sunday. We would spend the evening around the fireplace, with the family listening to the local chit-chat and contributing some of our own. Or, we would take the girl of the family to the movies. They were very hospitable people and we were a couple of boys uprooted from home, and trying not to be homesick.

You may ask, what has all this got to do with Pilot Training? Nothing, perhaps. But it has something to do with pilot survival. In some way this socializing took our minds off our sad condition back at the field. Of waiting for planes, and forced boondoggling—of attending unnecessary formations, policing the grounds, going on long hikes with packs. The Kiwis had orders to keep the men busy.

Then suddenly, unexpectedly, we had planes, if you want to call them that. They were Standards, with the Hall Scott four-cylinder truck engine, which we were to find very unreliable. The men were *on the line*, in company front to greet the sunrise, as usual. But this time there were ships. The ceremony of Reveille with the flag going up, roll call, the bugle playing was gone thru in the darkness and more quickly, while a row of thirty ships in their own company front, at right angles to ours, had been warming up in the darkness. Their motors throbbed a strange cacophony, in several tones, that even Gershwin could not imitate. Their exhausts glowed cherry red in the darkness, and that was about all you could see of them.

A sharp command from Sergeant Redmond and the men in company front broke and gathered in groups of eight around their assigned plane and instructor. A few words from the instructor and he climbed into the front seat of the plane, and the cadet into the rear. A mechanic pulled out the chocks, and the machine, with a snort or two, started moving slowly, sometimes by flashlight, toward the end of the runway.

As soon as it was possible to see the ground dimly, the instructor in the lead plane opened the throttle; the ships roared down the runway and lifted off. The dawn takeoff in the crisp Texas Air was to me terrifically impressive—something to remember both for its beauty and novelty. It always said something about the distant future of mankind. Bud was impressed but not very. His only comment was, "I wish it weren't so damn cold!"

Our first flights were really just rides, to get us used to being off the ground. Many of the cadets were "airsick" at first. And some few wet their pants from fright, which was considered a big joke and conversation piece. But a good instructor was by necessity a good psychologist and could build confidence so most of the men soon got over these weaknesses.

At first the instructor let the learner hold the stick—to push it slightly forward and back, then to one side and the other—to watch the responses of the ship. Then he demonstrated the different matter of the turn. He tried *not* to frighten the cadet, for they had been known to "freeze" out the stick and cause a crash. All this took place very gradually.

I was a little scared at first, but soon flying seemed quite natural. I put my mind to understanding the various instruments on the dash, and the throttle and the complicated combination of stick and rudder which make for a smooth turn. It was something that required thought and practice until one's responses became almost instinctive.

The first time is weird and wonderful. You climb into its seat thinking what a sinner you have been. You fasten the belt with about the same amount of acuity as you would in the electric chair. Your instructor, a matter-of-fact gentleman, executes the gymnastics necessary to getting into the front seat that is protected by a low "roof." He kicks around a few levers and hits your shins with the dual control. He fastens his helmet and adjusts his goggles with an exasperating finesse. A mechanic has been toying with the propeller. Suddenly:

"Off," says the instructor.

"Off," the mechanic repeats, and proceeds to do an Indian club revolution with the propeller. Eventually it comes to rest and he steps back.

"Contact," says the mechanic.

"Contact," repeats the instructor.

Something bangs up in front, the joystick suddenly comes to life and bangs back against the seat end. The mechanic gives the propeller a sharp turn and the motor picks up with a hollow but regularly punctuated sound. Two or three blasts of hot air and half-burned gasoline come back against your face.

The instructor looks back and upwards over his shoulders, and then over the top of the upper plane and between the wings to make sure that no other planes are landing. He looks back at you with the caressing glance of the death's head and the engine roars with the noise of seven cataracts and you jerk forward in your uncertain seat, sick at least for ever having left the city or township of your birth, and you wonder vaguely at the perverse ways of men and if the Kaiser knows the human agony he has caused.

* * *

Bud and I agreed that there was really not an awful lot to flying once you understood the controls and developed a sensitivity to the motions of the ship. This latter was called "flying by the seat of the pants." You could tell whether the ship was slipping sideways, whether it was going forward fast enough to hold the air. And if not, it would be falling directly downward bottom-side first (a sickening sensation which was called a stall). There existed corrections to all these things which must be learned so well as to become instinctive. Only then was a pilot "safe." Today, an unholy array of instruments on the dashboard of the big planes must be mastered, and the pilot no longer flies by the seat of his pants. But any old-time flyer will tell you the old way was much safer.

Most of the men developed a sensitivity to these things, but some few could not. Those that had no sensitivity at all were, sooner or later, killed in some senseless crash unless they were lucky enough to be detected in time and sent to the Balloon School. It was a pragmatic search for sensitivity. And that's why good instructors were so very important.

All this was really not as scary as it sounds. "Straight flying" exclusive of stunts is a mild sensation after the first two or three rides. The first loop or Immelmann is an unforgotten moment in the life of anyone who has ever flown. It is a moment when your heart rises to choke you, when your liver departs into space and the other organs, ordinarily considered necessary to the well-being of the human system, fly off at various tangents.

Training planes, especially the new Curtiss, were admirably designed for the beginning pilot. You held the stick in neutral, opened the throttle and she took off practically by herself. Once in the air you pulled back the stick a little to the proper rate of climb. Turns were a bit difficult at first because the pilot had to do four things together: lower the nose to level; push the stick to the left or right, which tipped up a wing; and pull the stick back carefully, coordinating it with the foot rudder. If you got the right combination, the ship turned nicely without slip or skid. Landings were for later on. But everything required much practice and keeping your head. The hidden truth was that the pilot taught himself thru intelligent experiment.

It normally took the men seven to eight hours of dual instruction in the primary stage, to "solo," that is, to go out alone, with the instructor on the ground. The Canadians at Taliaferro Field, Ft. Worth, soloed their men at three and four hours, but they had far too many accidents. I soloed at eight hours, and was very glad to leave my instructor and move to the advanced class. He was just as glad, too; for some reason we made each other nervous. After solo, we took advanced courses with other instructors—Cross Country, Aerobatics and Formation. At the end we were given a second lieutenant's commission and, far more important, the right to wear the wings. This happened to me in early August 1918.

In four and a half months' time we learned to fly—that is, those of us who escaped death or transfer to the balloons. It was fast by today's army or airline standards. And the Canucks were even faster. But it was not accomplished without cost. Our casualty rate was higher than the Infantry on the front. We had one or two deaths every week. And one week, four. At first there was a small military ceremony in which a formation of cadets accompanied the casket on a gun caisson to the field gates. I remember one week when an important cadet who was heir to a newspaper fortune in New York was killed. The whole field accompanied the body to town and filled the Episcopal Church. I can still hear the boy's young bride's uncontrollable screams during the ceremony.

After the day's flying was over, we made for the barracks to throw our leather coats and helmets on the cot, gather up soap, towel and razor and head for the noisy washroom to lose the grime of the day's work. This day I found Bud talking to a tall, blond, lanky fellow whose nose was literally hanging from his face.

"Cy, meet another Bud Fisher, from Patterson, Pennsylvania. Survivor of a recent crash!"

"Howdy, Cy. Just on my way to the hospital. Made a rather bad landing."

He was literally holding his nose on his face, but seemed very good natured about it. Further pleasantries were cut short by a man in a white coat who led him away.

Bud said, "He turned over in landing but I don't see how

he could break his nose. Couldn't be the stick hit him. He said he put his head on his arm like we are told to."

"It looked mighty painful," I said. "But he doesn't show it."

"He's an all-star tackle from Penn State. Or don't you read the papers?"

We adopted the second Bud into our social group of two. Henceforth he came to town with us on weekends, where he met most of the friends and acquaintances Bud and I had on the string. To avoid confusion we called him Floyd, which, after all, was his real name. He could take people or leave them alone, and had none of Bud's keenness for miscellaneous friendships. I think he enjoyed flying more than anything else. He was always a good and reliable friend to both of us. After the war the three of us corresponded until the end of our rather sad lives.

His nose was in time grafted back on, but it assumed a shape that was an anomaly to the rest of his face. It was broken in the middle and the lower half went in a swifter descent. He looked like the Dutch scholar Erasmus must have looked in his youth.

Floyd, being an Easterner, lacked our Middle West ebullience. He seemed too matter of fact and on the defensive, but never to us. He came from a poverty-stricken family in a small Dutch community, but had had the imagination to work his way through two years of the state university. He mentioned once that his brother was the town iceman.

After the war he emigrated to California, staying with me for a couple of weeks on the way. There he built workers' houses by the score and became a millionaire. He married twice but both were unsatisfactory liaisons. He had small patience with women. He died in middle age of some kind of deterioration of the arteries which interested him keenly as a medical problem while he was dying of it. I always think of him as a hell of a pilot. Today, were he alive, I can see him a top 747 commander, flying the world with the same nonchalance as of old—a thing which would be much more in character for him than building houses or being rich. But fate plays strange tricks.

About halfway through our training, the old "barn door" Standard airplane was discarded and we received the beautiful little Curtiss "Jenny" which we thought the ultimate ship. After that, cadet death was seldom attributed to mechanical failure. It was usually attributed to pilot error, plain bad luck, or to causes unknown. There were a few collisions in the air. Several bad landings. A couple of times a plane came down and landed on top of one waiting on the runway. One cadet, Richardson, rattled by something, lost his head completely and landed in a tree. He slid down the trunk and ran like hell just before the plane exploded. He lived, but never spoke again above a whisper. Vernon Castle, the famous dancer who had flown on the front with the RAF and was now an instructor, died trying to avoid a collision, near the ground, with a stupid cadet who had just soloed.

But to get back, once I had soloed successfully (that means without cracking anything), my instructor, Foote, turned in a paper that pronounced me competent in the air. After the usual delay, Bud and I stood side by side one day with a small group in the Commandant's office and swore again to bear true faith and allegiance to the United States against all its enemies. We were given commissions signed by the President, and the right to wear the silver wings. Automatically we joined the Officers' Club and Mess, where the food was much better. But there was a fly in the ointment. The men, so long together, were split up and sent to various fields. Bud to Ft. Sill to fly Reconnaissance and Artillery Spotting. I was to stay at Love and take a Pursuit course. I did not realize how much I was going to miss my old sidekick.

Love and Hicks

A fleet of flivvers conveyed the cadets from the field to town and back again at the end of their weekend holiday. The route in from the field at the foot of Ackard Street passed an emporium emblazoned with the sign—"Fine Monuments"—The

The photograph above was included in an original working manuscript of *Pilgrimage*.
(Courtesy of T.C. Corbett Family Archives)

yard sign in front of the establishment attested that the firm made not only fine monuments, but tombstones, headstones, footstones, mausoleums and all the other accoutrements of burial.

In passing this place there would always be some humorous and ribald comment, but every man in his heart secretly feared the day when he would have, for the first time, to fly to Hicks Field at Fort Worth. When the Royal Flying Corps had this field, they called it Taliaferro Field,[15] but when the Americans took it over some perverse fate had it called Hicks.[16]

As ill luck would have it, it came my turn to fly to Hicks on

---

15 The Canadians named the training complex Camp Taliaferro, after 1st Lieutenant Walter R. Taliaferro, a US Army aviator killed in an accident at Rockwell Field, California, on October 11, 1915.

16 Named after Charles Hicks, who had owned the land on which the airfield was built.

a Friday, the 13th.[17] Going through my leather coat to make sure that the rabbit foot was still there, I found thirteen cents in change. I left my ship while it was being gassed up, ran over to a little group of flyers and tried to borrow a few more rabbit feet. I might as well have tried to borrow one-way tickets to heaven.

Every fellow who had to fly that day hung tightly to his rabbit's foot, but to fly to Hicks! Well, there was nothing in the line of calamity that might not be expected from such a combination. Bud Fisher shook his head sadly and offered to fulfill any last request I might make. Failing there, I ran into the barracks and took one of the horseshoes hanging up over a door. When I got back to the ship, I opened the ship's toolbox and put the horseshoe in with the tools.

Fort Worth is some forty or fifty miles from Dallas and not hard to find if you pick up the right railroad out of Dallas and follow it conscientiously. We seldom if ever tried to fly by dead reckoning because the compasses were not reliable and because, to most flyers, Aerial Navigation as it was taught at the Field was a totally inexplicable science. An ex-professor taught the subject and took a fiendish and academic delight in dragging in so many complicating elements that nobody had any faith in the directions after they were plotted.

Finding the Fort Worth Railroad, I followed it carefully, watching all the while the water temperature and listening for a miss. Halfway to Fort Worth the sky began to cloud up—clouds were between seven and fifteen hundred feet. Noticing carefully the angle of the sun on my fuselage and the needle of the compass, I climbed above the clouds and attempted to fly by dead reckoning. The ground was visible in patches—only now and then, and it was not long before I had lost the railroad completely. After crossing fields, roads, hamlets and Interurban lines

---

17 September 13, 1918, was a Friday.

without number, I saw, through a break in the clouds, a large city beneath.

I throttled down and spiraled and side-slipped through the clouds, and then flew across Fort Worth in the direction of Hicks, which lay on the outskirts. I can still remember the sensation of sharp alarm which came to me as I approached the field. The motor had backfired once or twice, but ordinarily this was nothing. For no reason at all I cut the ignition switch and the motor stopped dead. I slipped to a gliding altitude and then glided in and landed safely. As the motor was not idling, I had no power to turn and taxi back across the field to the hangars. I sat there waiting for a motored mechanic to come out and crank the propeller. He came out, but instead of cranking her, he jumped out of the motorcycle side car, pyrene in hand, and sprayed a small fire under my engine! When it was out he showed me a seven-inch crack in the gasoline tank. Only a flyer can appreciate what luck that was.

The Adjutant of Hicks Field wired to Love and the answer came to repair the ship, and for me to wait for Lt. Campbell,[18] who would fly over to pick me up. I waited for him from 11:00 a.m. till 4:00 p.m. When he hadn't showed up, I started to town. I was a short way down the road, hiking to town, when I saw a ship glide in and land. I ran back as fast as I could, but before I arrived, he learned that I had started for town. As it was late, he started back immediately. I missed him by about two minutes.

On his way back to Love, Campbell had a forced landing and smashed up. While he was not seriously hurt, the front seat of his ship (where I would have been) was completely

---

18 Lt. William T. Campbell was a flight instructor at Love Field who gained national fame after he completed a world record of 151 consecutive loops on November 12, 1918.

Lt. William T. Campbell standing by his airplane following his record-breaking 151 consecutive loops at Love Field, Texas.
(Courtesy of DeGolyer Library, SMU, Texas: Photographs, Manuscripts, and Imprints.)

telescoped—engine back in the front seat's lap and the front and rear parts of the cowl smashed tightly together!

Oblivious of the fate I had so narrowly missed, I rode back to Dallas on the Interurban the next day, wondering how I would explain to the commandant why I wasn't on hand when Campbell stopped for me. But Major Netherwood never asked me why.

Random Notes:

I can remember a trip with mad Lt. Campbell where in taking off he flew directly at a barn until twenty feet away from it and then zoomed over it and swished through the top branches of young trees behind it. I was in the front seat, and it was the only indisputable, first-rate miracle that I ever witnessed. I can still recall the J.M.A. practice field with the aerial hurdles, its large bull's eye and its staked-off semicircles for practicing as close to the ground.

"Sick Semper"

A Kiwi—by the name of Captain Goetz—came to the field and was made adjutant. He was a lawyer. Because I am trying to keep this little account as truthful as possible, I called him a Kiwi, refraining from such expressions as a man, or a gentleman. But the exigencies of mixed reading prevent me from telling you what he really was. Men who were cadets will know what I mean. Never have I ceased to marvel at his lack of understanding of the men and at the great ill will he bore them. Some said he was in the pay of the German government, but others claimed that he had neither the brains nor the courage necessary to be a German agent.

Now, the average American (and these boys were representative of the best) is a tolerant animal. He minds his own business, does as much work as the exigencies of the case may require, and regards the human spectacle with an attitude that is somewhere between amusement and indifference. It is really hard to antagonize him. You may cheat him, disregard him, and even call him a nasty name (if you are a good enough friend) without raising his ire. There is only one thing you may *not* do. Don't try to frighten him.

From what I have read of their history, this intolerance of tyrants is the great outstanding characteristic of the Saxon strain, and all their achievements in government, it seems, are traceable to this source. Their genius is the genius of freedom, the humble right to live, unafraid.

The commandant of the field, Major O'Connell, a great, good-natured Irishman (none too perceptive, none too efficient, I suspect), turned over almost all of the administrative work to Goetz—who promptly instituted what might be mildly called a reign of terror.

He turned us out at 2 a.m. for fire drill four times in one week. He lengthened classes when the men were already worked to death and too tired to fly safely. He put a sick detail on police when the men should have gone to the hospital with influenza. He made us bail out cellars and pick up cigarette butts in our leisure moments. He tried to "bust" a few of the insubordinates. From those around him and from whomever had occasion to talk to him, he required the utmost in military obsequiousness.

The response to this treatment was electric. Goetz was instantly the most hated man I have ever seen. He was not even referred to as Goetz, but as "that————." Men would not salute him anywhere. In fact, nobody did, so he couldn't punish the whole field. At his own mess all decent fellows ostracized him, and even in town he was friendless. As the lowly cadets passed him in the lobby of the Adolphus, their lips would turn up in a sneer, where normally they would have saluted a good officer.

Then at the field a practice developed which became an institution and a tradition. As the men finished their courses and were commissioned, it was customary to invite Goetz, as an equal, to go for a ride. It was understood among the men that whoever got him in the air was bound to crash him.

The psychology of fear is a strange thing. These boys who saw death, who flew with it every day, could laugh at it. Were they afraid? The answer is no. Although there were terrific moments in the air when mortal flesh quaked and seemed unequal to the strain, these moments were quickly decided for life or for death and when past they were quickly forgotten. But Goetz, the groundhog, lived every day in mortal terror lest some order or circumstance would force him to go up. And he knew that day would see his finish. It is safe to say that if he succeeded, through his reign of terror—in frightening anyone—that person was himself.

Commanding officer and his staff, Love Field, 1917-1918. Standing, from left to right, are: Jack E. Duke, Russel Tower, Commanding Officer Major Albert L. Sneed, Norman Goetz, Frank Watson, and Ben H. Adams. Note that two officers aren't wearing wings: Goetz and Watson.
(Courtesy of DeGolyer Library, Southern Methodist University)

In all the time he was at Love, Goetz never got off the ground. I have heard, on fairly good authority, that one of the commissioned cadets beat him up directly after the Armistice was signed, and that another one met him a year later in New York and did the same thing. But this had always been the fate of tyrants among the sturdy men of North Europe.

"Cadet" blood (and I have often seen it spilled more than once) is the same blood that flowed at Agincourt and at Mons—at Cressy, at Hastings and at Ypres—blood of a race that has often known defeat but never slavery. The genius of other races may be art, empire or religion, but the genius of the Saxon will always be the genius of freedom—the humble right to live without fear. He had put down terror with the instruments of terror, and his tyrants have died in their cowardice.

SEVEN

The Sickening Sound of Silence

THESE EPISODES MAY SEEM BADLY ORDERED, but they detailed an enlargement of some period of Pilot Training which is itself an overall and perhaps too rapid picture of our life as amateur soldiers. This scene is laid in the time when we still had the old Standards and were struggling manfully to master the old "flying barn doors."

It was obvious to one and all that these ships were ill-designed; too little power, too much wing surface and moderate controls. The Standard was literally a mess, put together in a hurry by men who didn't have to fly them. They were a mortal danger to beginning pilots, and instructors, and the opinion was you had to be lucky to survive.

This was the ship I soloed on, after sixteen forced landings. And as I look back now, I don't blame old Foote, my timid but irascible instructor, for being mortally scared of me, the ship, and everything else. The power plant was a heavy four-cylinder engine called the Hall-Scott, of about 100 horsepower. It was designed for trucks and far too heavy for the air. But when one cylinder cut out, usually without warning, the pilot had no alternative but to come down fast, no matter what he was over. I had sixteen forced landings before the crash, an excellent record.

Learning pilots landed on everything that was there, including trees and Bockman's Dam, and the grounds of S.M.U. (Southern Methodist University). Many were killed. Innumerable ships damaged or destroyed. Forced landing techniques fast became an added branch of the curriculum, and many of the men became very skilled at it.

The thing was to be aware at all times of what terrain you were over and which way to turn, and, most of all, how far to stretch a glide to reach a flat field. Cotton fields and flat pastures were the best, except for hog wallers and hidden streams. Fences were also deadly because they often could not be discerned until too late. The alert pilot always knew which was the best way to turn when he first heard the ominous sound of silence. Then he prayed that luck was still with him.

The Standard was a biplane with a too-large wing spread. Struts separated the wings vertically. And crossed guy wires with turnbuckles made the whole section rigid. The wings lifted up slightly from the body in a thing called a dihedral, and for safety there was an inch or so of play in the rigging of the wings to the fuselage. Planes today are monoplanes with no struts or guying and have an immensely stronger structure with steel longerons. The old Standard with its low horsepower and high wing spread could be buffeted about like a leaf in a storm. And often was. It was a scary machine.

I remember that pleasant afternoon when Dave Lutz (a glutton for flying time) turned over his ship to me gratuitously. It aroused my suspicion. Nevertheless, I gassed her up and took off. I was not outside the field very far before my worst suspicions were confirmed—the engine began to miss. When one cylinder in four started to cut out, there was only one thing to do and that was to look for a soft spot and land. I slid over telephone wires into a short and narrow field of young grain and put her down without cracking. A mechanic in a motorcycle found me after a half hour, and after another half hour of assiduous tinkering announced that the ship was O.K. and ready to go.

I cranked her and chanced a takeoff with the wind. I was not fifty feet over the aforementioned telephone wires when the motor cut out completely. I nosed down sharply and told God I was sorry for all my sins.

A "Standard" sits quietly in a field after one of Corbett's many forced landings.
(Courtesy of T.C. Corbett Family Archives)

After hopping a road and a fence, I surprised myself by coming to a safe standstill between two houses. The mechanic came up, with his driver, after a bit, and explained how sorry he was for forgetting to reinsert the auxiliary jet of my carburetor after cleaning it. No offense meant, he said, and hoped I had taken none. It was quite all right, I told him, and after this exchange of amenities I *watched* him put the jet where it belonged.

I cranked up again and took off, this time gaining a hundred feet when she started to miss badly. There was a patch of woods and rolling "hog waller" ground ahead and beneath me, but by main force and determination I held her up for a minute or two till I gained a nice wheat field into which I slid and put her down without any trouble.

The industrious M.S.E. found me again and explained that his former diagnosis had been all wrong—the plane had ignition trouble instead of carburetor trouble. That man certainly had the abstract ways of an academician.

It took him an hour and a half to fix the magneto and at that, he explained to me, it really was not a workmanlike job but would do to get the ship back to the field where it could be fixed properly.

At that I balked a little and suggested that the ship had better be wheeled in than smashed altogether. But he said if I didn't take it in, he would have to guard it all night. I relented and decided to take a chance, as Love was only a half-mile away.

Pilgrimage, 1923
Yesterday I was out near the old red high-school house, south of Love Field, which was witness to my first and only crash. I found the road and the very spot where I put one of Love Field's flying coffins (the old Standards) permanently out of service.

After solo, we were assigned to "Cross-Country." That meant flying to some designated town nearby, landing, eating a box lunch, gassing up, receiving a quick inspection by a mechanic, and flying home. That was the ideal flight plan not too often achieved.

This day I was to fly to the little town of Denton, about fifteen miles away. The town had a landing field, lunch facilities, gas trucks and two or three mechanics with tools for minor repairs (and not much knowledge of what they were doing). It was a distinct achievement for a cadet to make the round trip without mishap.

I wasn't two minutes in the air before I knew the machine I had was a lemon. The motor didn't sound right. It was regular, but there was a low-pitched whine added. I was maybe five or six miles out from the field when the engine cut out altogether, leaving only the horrible sound of silence. And silence was a shock after the unharmonic racket it had been making.

I looked around quickly and spotted a nice cotton field straight ahead—no obstructions, no fences, no streams or forest patches. I lowered the nose and side-slipped to the proper altitude and came down and landed smoothly. I shut off the engine and proceeded to wait. Soon a couple of mechanics and their noisy motorcycle sidecar appeared and started to tinker with the engine.

"We have it, Sir. Just a fouled spark plug and timing a little off. You can take her up now."

One of them turned the propeller in the ritual of starting.

And the deep-throated roar was going again. It sounded pretty good, I thought, but then, I was not much of a judge.

One man held the wing while I turned and taxied to the far end of the field and turned again into position for takeoff. I opened the throttle; she bounced a few times and was in the air. "This time I'll make it," I told myself.

The Crash

There was a little patch of woods to my right. I turned to go over it to correct my direction of flight to Denton. I was over the woods and perhaps 150 feet in the air when there was suddenly another horrible silence. I was too low to risk a turn without power but it looked like I could stretch the glide over the rest of the woods to a clear field beyond.

I almost made it. I stretched the glide pretty thin and had gotten clear of the main woods. I nosed down sharply but not soon enough, for the ship was stalling, and at that moment I knew with a complete conviction that I was going to crash. In two counts I threw off my goggles, cut the ignition switch and made a pillow for my head with my arms on the cowl.

She crashed. There was a terrific yank on my stomach from the belt and I can still hear the splintering wood after that fifty-foot dive into the road. We were nose down into a hard Texas road. The left wing hit first and then the ship's nose dug in. The fuselage was almost perpendicular, and it teetered a second or two and then fell back on its chassis. After the noise abated I waited a second, decided that I was unhurt as I could feel no pain, and then climbed out.

Old 1645 was a sorry mess. Both wings and prop and landing gear stove-in, and the engine back in the front seat's lap. The ship resembled a winged duck that has just fallen apart.

I sat on the bank of a ditch by the roadside, contemplating the wreckage until the mechanics came up in their noisy motorcycle.

"You hurt, Sir?"

"No, I guess not."

"Lucky! It couldn't have been the timing. But she sure is a mess now. Sure you're all right?"

"I guess so," I said, and then passed out.

Next thing I knew I was in the sidecar speeding back to the Field and the hospital. The doctors pronounced me unhurt except for shock, and ordered two days' rest. I was also summoned to the Commandant's office where I signed a paper saying that I didn't do it on purpose. So now, dear reader, you know how to crash successfully, and no doubt will do so as long as you possess its one and only requisite—luck, and lots of it.

Cy Corbett standing by his wrecked plane (1918).
(Courtesy of T.C. Corbett Family Archives)

"Lady Luck"[19]

If there were any flyers in the Air Service who were not superstitious, they must have been the ones I didn't meet. Never in that year and a half did I see three flyers light cigarettes on one match. When Friday came on the thirteenth there was no flying time put in that could be avoided. Many of the men carried talismans or good luck tokens. The commonest charm was, possibly, the left hind foot of a rabbit carried in the upper left-hand pocket of the flying coat. Some men actually carried horseshoes in their pockets or hung them up over their bunks. Others carried some small trinket belonging to a flyer known for his luck. (Such a one was Abie Faneuf.)

---

19 In December 1925 Cy Corbett had pieces of his recollections of army life printed in *The Trib*, the in-house publication for employees of the *Chicago Tribune*, and read on the air at WGN radio.

Things, persons, events known to bring on hard luck were carefully avoided. Certain of the men were unlucky in regard to each other but all right as regards everyone else. Such an unluckful combination were Dave Lutz and I. The only ship I ever smashed was one he turned over to me on the second solo stage. He similarly crashed one I gave him.

One day an instructor by the name of Adams was all ready to take me out to practice forced landings at the Preston Road field. I was strapped in, had helmet and goggles on. He, in the front seat, had tested the motor to his satisfaction. Before taking off he looked again at his list of cadets and saw that it was really Lutz's turn instead of mine. He told me. I got out and Lutz got in. They took off.

I followed them fifteen minutes later with another instructor. There they were—smashed badly from a tailspin. Adams broke both legs; Dave gave his back a nasty wrench.

Dave Lutz, University of Illinois Ground School.
(Courtesy of T.C. Corbett Family Archives)

Months later on the formation stage I was practicing close flying with Requa as instructor. Suddenly he took the ship from my control, dropped out of the formation and landed in a field where another plane had been forced down. It was Lutz. We helped him as best we could and left. Before reaching the field we developed a miss and had to land. Although Requa was thought to be the best flyer at the field, and despite some neat zooming of wires and hopping of fences, he couldn't stop before smashing into a fence and damaging the ship. Lutz and I were mutually poisonous for luck, and needless to say carefully avoided each other.

* * *

Anything belonging to a dead man was rotten luck. When Zinn and Insinger crashed in the air, Insinger was killed instantly[20] and Zinn was expected to die. When the wrecking crew hauled in the wrecked planes, I took a little bronze turnbuckle from each, thinking to give them to Zinn, if perchance he should live. I put them in my trunk.

Now, I knew better than to do this.

The next day was payday. Through some clerical error there was no pay for me. This was very depressing.

The following day Instructor Foote, in the front seat, and I were making the first turn down near the machine shops when the motor cut out. He grabbed the controls, narrowly missed a smokestack, banked her around and tried to land with a stiff wind under his tail. We gained more ground speed in this descent than we had with the motor.

We must have been going 100 miles an hour while Foote

---

20 Cadet John Insinger of Greenleaf, Colorado, was killed at Love Field April 9, 1918, when two machines crashed, about five hundred feet in the air. According to the *El Paso Herald* of April 9, 1918, the pilot of the other plane, Earl Lynn (not Zinn), was "slightly injured."

held her a few feet off the ground and prayed for a stop. We were rapidly approaching the T. We crossed it and went hell bent down a narrow lane between two lines of ships that were being repaired or gassed. I thought we were going right on through the side of the hangar, but we finally did stop with not any too much room to spare.

Foote couldn't walk for a few minutes. Some of the boys waved back the meat wagon (ambulance), and started the usual line of ragging.

Foote flew no more that day.

I could see in his eye that Foote was leery of my luck the next day, as I climbed in for more instruction in the art of the eagle. The wind was opposite. We were taking off over the hangars instead of toward the machine shops. We were about 200 feet over Hangar 9 and preparing for the first turn. Whatever made me do it I don't know, but I threw the ship into a vertical bank with her nose in the air. (I had been listening to the boys in the barracks "bunk flying" about crossing controls in vertical banks.) As we turned into the wind we rapidly lost flying speed and started to stall. Foote, who had been daydreaming a little, I guess, grabbed the controls and saved the situation. When we landed he ordered me out of the ship. He turned me in to the officer in charge of flying, Captain Dodd.

That afternoon Dodd had me up on the carpet and told me he was going to "bust" me before I killed myself and one of his instructors. Not that it mattered much about the former, he said, but good instructors were hard to get.

I talked hard and fast for five minutes, trying to tell him that I had made a mistake anyone might make and had no intention of killing Foote. He finally let me off with confinement to the post until commissioned, as punishment.

That night I took a walk down the road and tossed the turnbuckles into an adjacent ditch. The next day I turned in Insinger's helmet (he had borrowed mine) for a new one.

Shortly after that my pay came through. Foote and I had

no more forced landings, but it took a long time for him to become convinced that I had no intentions against his life.

**

Finsterwald spun down 400 feet and smashed up in the chicken yard of one of the many "chicken dinner" roadhouses around Dallas. When the plane finally stopped, amid great chicken carnage and a cloud of white feathers, he was unhurt and unscratched. But he neglected to knock wood, and in trying to get down from the cockpit, through the wreckage of the machine and the tangle of chicken wire, he broke his leg and scratched his hands and face on the cut wire.

Motorcycle drivers (enlisted men) at the field had a habit of riding along with the wheel of the sidecar a foot or so off the ground. A flyer by the name of De Learie, who had crashed many times without a scratch, was riding from town with one of these two-wheel drivers. The driver forgot to put the wheel down before turning a corner. The motorcycle did an Immelmann, throwing De Learie against a fence post and breaking his arm. He had left his rabbit foot at the field, in his flying coat.

So far as I have been able to ascertain, the only flyers who don't believe in luck are the dead ones.

And there was Bisbinghoff, the unluckiest man on the field. And nothing could change his luck. It was said that every time he went up he cracked something, if it were only a wing skid. He washed out four or five ships and damaged several others in a greater or lesser degree before the brass hats decided that he had better be eliminated before he killed himself. So they sent him to be an observer.

Before he was finally discharged he was flying in a five-ship formation one day, and he was flying the fifth ship, which is a hard position for a skilled and lucky pilot. The leader signaled for a left-hand turn whereupon the second and third ships cut diagonally into position without trouble. Mead Terry, in the fourth ship, slowed down to the stalling point, waiting for them, and Bisbinghoff ran him over. Seeing him in line he zoomed up sharply until he was directly over Terry. In pulling up he stalled and started to slash down into Terry's ship. He put one of the wheels of his landing chassis through Terry's center section, smashing it, wood and canvas all to bits excepting two slender brass wires, which were all that kept Terry's upper wings from caving in. Terry slowed up, coasted down gently from 5,000 feet and finally put the ship on the ground. But it was an anxious descent and to me the wonder is that Terry didn't die of heart failure from the suspense of wondering at what moment his wings would come off.

Bisbinghoff had innumerable forced landings from engine trouble—a thing for which he was in no way responsible. But the circumstance which finally busted him was this: One day on cross-country flying Bisbinghoff developed a miss, but right over a beautiful flat field in which there were no trees, no dividing fences, no riverlets—flat as a billiard table. With such a prospect before him, a pilot could almost close his eyes and land. Bisbinghoff thought that now for once he would bring down his ship without cracking it. He figured the wind, maneuvered for right position, glided in and landed—but on a cow, the only living thing—the only obstacle—in that 160-acre field. The cow was killed. The propeller was broken. The farmer collected damages and Bisbinghoff got orders to an observation squadron.

***

Toward the end of my first day's "rest," which consisted mainly of bunk fatigue on my own cot in the barracks, Fisher appeared in his only flying clothes and asked,

"How are you feeling, Cy?"

"All right, Bud."

"Can you come for a little walk? I want to show you something."

We strolled leisurely down the company street to the region of the immense hangars where seven or eight planes were stored overnight.

In an open space behind one of them was the junk pile, where crashed planes were put, awaiting the salvage crews who took off metal parts and gathered up the rest for burning. There I saw #1647—the plane I had crashed—with its broken wings detached. It was a sorry mess.

"It's mine, all right," I said.

"See the one next to it? That's the one Zinn was killed in last week."[21]

It did not seem nearly as badly smashed as mine.

"What you got, you lucky Irishman?" Bud asked.

"Must have been my Guardian Angel on the stick," I said.

Bud gave me one of his more skeptical looks through his tough-guy expression and replied:

"No chance. It's just the confounded luck of the Irish, you lucky stiff!"

I thought myself it was phenomenally lucky. But then I firmly believed in my luck, as every flyer did, until his luck ran out.

It was not until the War was over and I was back home trying on civilian life for size that I had inklings that my first and only crash was not perhaps as lucky as I thought.

---

21 Zinn actually survived the crash, but for some time afterward, his fellow cadets expected him to die. Insinger was the cadet actually killed in the collision.

EIGHT

The Good Companion

I CAN STILL SEE HIS PLEASANT, BULLDOG FACE. Bud Fisher was by no means handsome. He had a jutting jaw, and his jowls were darkened by tomorrow's beard. He was of very even temper, with a keen sense of humor and a ready laugh. He looked very aggressive but he was a surprisingly mild person. And he grew on you.

He was the youngest of two sons of a coal mine owner and operator in downstate Illinois. His mother had been dead for years. His father had sent him through four years of Dartmouth[22] and given him a Stutz Bearcat to play with. Through Dartmouth he knew many of the important families in the East. But Bud was no snob. He liked everybody. He was interested in everybody, but the love of his life was Norma Talmadge, the movie star whom he had never met. He believed that education was something you had to put up with in order to get a good place in life. But otherwise, a big bore. He was conservative, intelligent and full of wonderful common sense that seemed pointed mainly

---

22 Fisher may have attended Dartmouth, but a Ewing Benedict Fisher from Springfield, Illinois, is listed in the 1917 edition of *The Gulielmensian*, a publication of Williams College, in Massachusetts.

at survival. His whole family was as Republican as they come. He was now going through the arduous and dangerous training of an army pilot, -not to save the world for Democracy, but simply because it seemed the thing to do.

The father and two sons lived in Springfield, Illinois, in a large, rambling old house, with servants, and were regarded as the pillars of the community.

I first met Bud when I was assigned a cot next to his in the barracks at Love, when we first moved from Camp Dick. He was doing "bunk fatigue" but quickly arose, came over and introduced himself, saying with a grimace, "We are going to be neighbors so we may as well be friends."

Men without women tend to find a pal, a partner or sidekick of their own sex in accordance with some obscure instinct that first brought the cavemen together in a defensive union. How well their temperaments meshed determines how well they get on and how long the friendship lasts. There was nothing wrong or sinful in their friendships. And we would have been thoroughly shocked at the modern notion that there could be. Bud was a great pal. He was never downcast. He was never demanding. He could always see the funny side of some idiotic army order. He was very social, and really loved people. He kept me from being homesick, which most of the men were, very, at this stage of their adventure. He could have written the book on how to survive in a strange environment.

The only transportation into Dallas from the field were "jitneys"—beat-up old Fords, without a top, into which the enterprising driver crowded as many as seven cadets at twenty-five cents each. Then a fast and hair-raising run into the city which was about eight miles away. We usually got off at the Adolphus Hotel, proceeded to the bar and had an *Adolphus coke*, a small sweet drink which was very satisfying. I never found a thirst anywhere to compare with one worked up in the semiarid Texas air. Nor a drink anywhere to compare with the Adolphus coke.

And, it was nonalcoholic. The men were lined up three and four deep along the bar, and it was a pandemonium of noisy good fellowship. Thirst satisfied, we would depart singly or in pairs for various destinations. But for most it was usually a lonesome weekend.

    We could go back to the Field for the night but we usually stayed in town at one of the less pretentious hotels that made the flying cadets a rate. The height of luxury, of course, was to stay at the Adolphus, sleep late and have one of their deluxe breakfasts. Bud and I heard about it only because we never had that kind of money. We did not pick up stray girls although the town teemed with them. However, many of the men did, more out of loneliness than lust.

    The line of demarcation among the men was surprisingly a moral one. There were those who always stayed with a girl on weekends. And those who did not. Bud and I both thot this weekend cohabitation very wrong, and did not indulge in it. He had been raised a strict Episcopalian and I a Catholic. Whenever we ran into one of the loose lovers in town with a good-looking girl in tow, we told ourselves she wasn't very attractive and a little on the dowdy side. We tried not to envy them, and not to think of the fun we were missing while trying to keep our souls in shape for a quick call to Valhalla.

    This day Bud and I had nothing to do and were sauntering aimlessly down the main street of Dallas when he spied something in a shop window. He was a born city man and loved to "spot" things. It was a photographer's window displaying busts of gallant young gentlemen in aviators' helmets and goggles. The faces had been cleverly retouched to give them a brave and patriotic appeal. Nothing would satisfy Bud but that we had to go inside and have ourselves idealized. We ordered half a dozen prints each, which we picked up the following weekend. They were handsome, 12x18 enlargements.

Cy Corbett, 1918.
(Courtesy of T.C. Corbett Family Archives)

We spent some thought and decision on what girls to send them to, outside the family. I sent one to Mother, one to my sister, and one to Sis Walsh. The remaining three went to girls I knew in Chicago, none of whom was a serious love. Little did I foresee the consequences. Bud distributed his in much the same way—one to his father, one to his brother, Reed, and one to the glamorous movie queen he did not know. The remaining went to girls he knew casually in Dallas. Actuated by patriotism, or some emotion rife in wartime, both sets of girls tended to make a much bigger thing of the gifts than we ever intended. We might as well have sent them engagement rings. In letters from home, shortly, I was appalled to find myself engaged to three different girls, when I well knew my heart belonged to Sis.

Some weeks later, during an idle afternoon in town, Bud

did some further spotting. I should have learned my lesson, but Bud was a terrific salesman when possessed by an idea. This time it was in a jeweler's window—beautiful, miniature silver wings, in the exact design of a pilot's insignia, but about half size. I think it was their beauty I couldn't resist. They were quite expensive, but we bought three each and dispatched them to girls, but not the same girls as the pictures. This Bud mysteriously insisted on and I could not figure why at the time. The effect was even more disastrous. In certain quarters I was years living down the reputation of an irresponsible Lothario. One lovely creature whom I happened to meet again, just a year before she died, showed me the silver wings which she had kept through the following fifty-two years. I was conscience-stricken. I wrote to Bud and asked him why he had done it. He said he guessed he was just an amateur psychologist experimenting on female reactions.

Writing this in my old age, I have pondered his youthful wisdom. Bud did not want to change the world. He liked it the way it was, reluctantly admitting that it had some imperfections, but they did not bother him. He liked girls socially but was never very much in love. He thought picking a wife a very serious matter which he would get around to some time later. He was really an arch conservative, not looking for trouble, but rather intent on avoiding it. Later, when I met his father and brother, they were exactly the same way. So I figured it was something in the genes.

In the course of a long life he was married twice, and got on congenially with each one. He had one child, a daughter. But mostly he achieved a life almost free from anxiety and regret. He worked for the same firm all his life and made a very comfortable if not spectacular living. He had no big troubles or personal disaster. To me he is proof of a middle-of-the-road wisdom that the Latin poet Horace so highly recommended.

One time when I visited him briefly in Mount Vernon, Illinois, he lived in a beautiful old house full of costly antiques which his second wife, a lovely young French girl, had collected. In the barn were two late Cadillacs. When I asked him how things were going he replied, "Pretty good, except I can't save any money." The two Fishers and I had corresponded off and on for years, and when I wrote and told the other Bud Fisher (who lived in California) what he said, Bud the second replied, "Anybody who has all that stuff doesn't need to save money!"

But this is my outstanding memory of Bud, after all these years: a big grin on his pleasant, bulldog face which was smeared with engine oil, as was his leather jacket and helmet, goggles on the top of his head. He was watching a Jennie roar down the runway in the early dawn, and said, "Golly, Cy, they'll never, *never* make a better ship than these little ole Jennies!"

When one thinks of the huge airplane of the present—the 727s and the 747s that cost $25,000,000[23] to build and can carry three hundred passengers to Europe—truly mechanical monsters, leviathans of the air, one had to admit that Bud was not much of a prophet.

Nevertheless my strongest memory of World War I, of all the hundreds of incidents, people and curiosities of the period, was Bud's honest, bulldog face, wreathed in a jubilant grin of deep affection for the lovely "Jennie," the Curtiss model number JN-4D which cost the government about $10,000 and which price we thought an outrageous gyp—of the taxpayer.

I think I ought to say a word about another friend of the period, Leslie R. Gray. He was the man on the nearby bunk reading a scientific journal and looking annoyed. I still see his lean and hungry face. He was tall, thin, dark and very intelligent. He had two degrees in mathematics and was an instructor at the University of Illinois. He came from a farm home near Bloomington and was always a little grumpy. Bud and I dragged him to town a few times but he didn't go over well with the

---

23 Cy's estimate in 1970.

ladies—although he was much better looking than either of us. Bud looked like a friendly bulldog. (And I had fiery red hair and the map of Ireland all over my face.) It demonstrated plainly to me how important Bud's know-how was. Gray often stayed in the barracks over the weekend, catching up on his damn scientific journals. Bud regarded him as a hopeless case of dourness. However, while the three of us had adjoining bunks we always muscled him along to town and did what we could to cheer him up. He was a born pessimist and didn't enjoy life; he got to be a pretty good flyer and stayed the course.

Bud belonged to a different group and had a different flying instructor. Some of them were 1st lieutenants, some civilian instructors. My own was Henry Foote, a civilian, short, heavyset and gruff. He was rated by the men as a "nervous Nellie," one not at ease in the air, and who didn't like cadets. Such instructors were regarded as a piece of bad luck.

Flying usually lasted about five hours, for after 10 a.m. the air got too "thin" and was dangerous for beginners. The controls were less effective. It could resume after four, and often did, when we needed flying time.

Bud Fisher had a very similar experience which he took matter-of-factly, and with wry Republican comments on almost everything, but especially on the ineptness of the government's teaching methods. But he thoroughly enjoyed flying and soon became very good at it.

I left Chicago November 24, 1917, for Ground School at the University of Illinois that took two months. We arrived at Dallas and Camp Dick, and were uncomfortable there for about six weeks. Early in March we were sent to Love Field on about the 15th, and there, we started to fly. I soloed, and was commissioned a second lieutenant with a pilot's rating early in August. That was when Bud and I were separated. He was assigned to Fort Sill, Oklahoma. I stayed on at Love, taking the Pursuit training course, and doing advanced flying until I broke my way out of the jam of pilots, thru a stint at army journalism. I got my overseas orders early in November, and was off for Hoboken, the port of embarkation.

Pilots

Every man believed firmly in his own luck until shown otherwise. It was thought that if a man "lost his nerve" he was as good as dead unless he requested immediately to be taken off flying, which few did. Everything was done to protect the men's morale. And a flying instructor who became jittery, and showed it, was quickly relieved. But the cadets who lashed thru and finally got their wings were never quite the same again. It did something to the nervous system. And their subsequent lives showed it in many ways— callousness toward life and death or in hard drinking. Or, in a total lack of ambition.

After primary training, the solo, wings and commission, came secondary or R.M.A. training for some of us. It consisted of advanced acrobatics, doing figure 8s with one wing almost dragging the ground, landing on a target and a lot of other dangerous nonsense that some non-flyer had thought of. Many were killed in boondoggles. Our Air Force in Europe had its own Pursuit training fields in England. There were 8,000 young pilots in the U.S. trained and raring to go and not enough planes abroad. Through some miscalculation of the brass a great many competent flyers never got near their overseas orders. (I did thru sheer luck, John Dewey and Army journalism.)

Through an intelligent grapevine the pilots knew all this but stolidly did what they were told, no matter how dangerous or exasperating. They tried hard to be good soldiers and to follow orders which often seemed to be issued by nitwits. They knew the war was winding to a close and that they were likely to miss the greatest show of the century. The thought of their own death never occurred to them, which shows how huge the morale was.

Almost all of the officers in charge of our training—first lieutenants, captains, majors, and an occasional colonel—were peewees: that is, they were commissioned officers without the wings. They were ninety-day wonders, country lawyers, or out-and-out political appointees. Seldom were we given a West Pointer or a career army man. The cadets were without exception college men, many from the Ivy League colleges, and the difference showed. They were far more intelligent and had more life, education and savvy than their commanders. The situation made for a good deal of exasperation all around.

During these four to five months our training went through the various stages: Flying, Landings, Cross Country, Acrobatics, Gunnery and Formation. We were absorbed in the lore of the pilot's craft and almost forgot our personal lives. The instructors were our heroes. They knew so much about the esoteric business. It never occurred to us that the next day might be our last. We had lost all fear of death. Men just dropped out and disappeared, like pawns in a chess game.[24]

Bud Fisher took all this admirably and in stride, with many a wisecrack and wry comment that renewed my faith in democracy. He was the solid, sensible citizen, backbone of the country, keeping his head through any crisis. I developed a great admiration for him. There was a large strain of New England in his makeup and it was instinctive. It gave me to understand that democracy is the last stage in the evolutionary process of human society. And after us, the Deluge.

Random Thoughts

These were the most interesting, most educative five months of my life. It was not so much the training in flying as the contact with intelligent and educated young Americans and their joyful outlook and enterprise. It was this which has made our country

---

24 According to *The Whitewright Sun*, a Texas paper, 106 pilots in training were killed at the three Ft. Worth training fields, which produced 1,475 "finished aviators." At Love Field, another twenty were killed during the training years 1918–1919. (Source:http://www.accident-report.com/USN/world/namerica/slist/love.html)

the most forward looking in the world, as well as the wealthiest. My only regret is that I had neither the time nor money to look them up in afterlife, and to study how they fared.

Nothing much happened during those five months, yet everything happened. We learned to move about an alien element. We got a new and amazing view of man, his works, his life, and his relation to the world, -one that had never been seen before, except by a few balloonists. It was unsettling to college youths. It was enough to affect a man's whole outlook on life. And that's what it did.

The Air Force soon taught me that there was a great deal more to life than what you learned in Plato and Thomas à Kempis. The world had changed vastly due to man's inventions, but I could not believe that man himself had changed much. The ground rules still looked the same; man was a frail chemical mechanism that flourished a while, in a favorable environment, then gradually deteriorated until his mechanism ran down altogether and they put him underground, mostly to protect the living. But the important thing was, he had a soul. The soul developed and flourished or withered and died, according to his good works and generosity, while on earth according to his selfishness and lusts. You had two things in delicate balance. But the soul and what happened to it on its earthly tour of duty was by far the most important; for our Father in heaven would accept into paradise only clean and healthy souls. That's what we were taught and believed.

The Army and the intelligent young gentlemen in it threw a different light on these things. A theological discussion I never heard. But one picked up from the men's attitude and conversation that such things were totally unimportant, if indeed they existed at all. The important thing was the here and now, one's continued survival, in health, happiness and some degree of wealth. One should not be an obvious stinker, but anything short of that was probably O.K. One should get the lead out of one's naturally lazy ass, achieve a good job, and find a nice-looking girl to sleep with. The rest of the categorical imperatives were nonsense.

Lastly, there was no sense at all in worrying about death. Nobody knows what happens afterwards. Very likely nothing. This philosophy, I noticed regretfully, seemed to free a man from a lot of his subconscious anxieties. I tried to adopt this into my own thinking, in order to become more fully one of the boys whose joyous approach to life I was beginning to admire greatly.

I met men along the way who taught me the practical arts of the country. Among them, not an ulcer or an incipient nervous breakdown in a carload. But there was a high degree of native skill and friendliness. They were inclined to be suspicious of people who inadvertently used words not in their ordinary vocabulary. But in my case, they overlooked the slips and put me down as a well-intentioned city nut. And so they helped me learn the skills of survival.

***

Recollection:

"Old Soldiers never, never dies;
They awnly fides awhy-"
—from "Mandalay" by Kipling

Portraits of a Few Old Soldiers
Leslie Gray, Abie Faneuf, Herrin, The Duke

Leslie Gray

Successful flying, they say, is made up of luck and intuition. Abie Faneuf was an example of the luck school, while Leslie Gray stood for the intuitive. Gray was a boy with a good set of brains and strong native judgment; but neither brains nor judgment could account for some of his escapes, for there is nothing else to ascribe them to than intuition.

Leslie Gray, University of Illinois Ground School
(Courtesy of T.C. Corbett Family Archives)

Thinking back to the old days, I can see many pictures of Gray, a lean, dark figure standing in the rain when he was stage commander, calling the roll of his outfit of thirty-five, and with three present, answering, "All present and accounted for, sir." I see him struggling with an old Standard about thirty feet off the ground, trying to put it down and finally stalling and wiping off the landing chassis. I can see him on that day when we, half dead from overwork and little rest, crawled into an empty airplane crate and went to sleep. But these were minor adventures.

In April 1918 Gray had soloed and was on the stage where you fly around the field, make a landing and then fly around again and so on, ad infinitum. Although everything was apparently all right with the ship, Gray didn't like it. After a few times around he gave it up to the next cadet in line—Earl Zinn, who flew it around his allotted time and then returned it to Gray. Gray had concluded that he was a little nervous that morning, so took off again and tried to forget his fears. After twice around he was more convinced than ever that something was wrong, although the motor hit steadily, with never a miss, and the controls responded quickly. He called the Dodo instructor, a sort of universal troubleshooter for nervous flyers. The Dodo man got in the front seat and took the ship around twice and pronounced it entirely O.K. Gray went around once more by himself, then got out and gave the ship up to Zinn.

On this stage the field was always crowded, and one had to watch his chance to turn and land. On his third or fourth time around Zinn was about to turn left and glide in. Another plane ahead of him and to his right was already turning left and thus crossing his temporary line of flight. When Zinn tried to bank and turn, the controls were locked tight and before he could move them an inch he had driven full speed into the other machine. From the ground I saw the collision, saw the locked fuselages fall. Bits of broken wood and torn canvas and a severed aileron fluttered down long after the main wreckage had hit the ground.

Insinger,[25] the man in the other plane ahead, was killed instantly and mutilated by Zinn's propeller. Zinn, thought dead, was taken to the morgue where it was discovered that he was still alive. He spent six months in the hospital and then came back to flying.

Later a mechanic was found who said that Gray's and Zinn's fatal ship had been taken out of the shop by mistake before it was released. The fuselage brace wires were all slack and the ship was out of true. This is the ship that Leslie Gray, against all reason, had refused.

* * *

At the field at West Point, Mississippi, was a commandant who believed in putting in flying time, rain or shine. So he

---

25 Cadet John W.A. Insinger is listed in Army records as dying at Love Field on April 9, 1918, while flying an SJ-1, Serial Number AS-4720.

ordered a gravel patch, a strip about 25 feet wide and long enough to take off on. It was a drizzly day and the boys were taking off from the "Gravel Patch." Gray was in the air with the cold rain beating in his face and feeling distinctly uncomfortable. After forty-five minutes of flying he decided for no reason at all to return to the field and land. He missed the first attempt, as a ship was just taking off from the gravel. He went around the field again with the feeling that he must land the next time. Another ship had taxied out to the rear end of the patch and again obstructed his landing. Gray cut the throttle and moved her down in a sharp descent. When he came to the ship that was in his way, he executed a neat bit of flying—a skid left and a skid right, putting her wheels down on the gravel right in front of the other ship. This double skid was an extremely dangerous thing to do close to the ground with a low-powered training ship. A puff of wind would have meant death and disaster, and Gray, as he got out, wondered why he had done it. Two mechanics ran past him with pyrene extinguishers, threw open the cowl, and put out a fire under the engine.

I had dinner with Gray and his wife last evening at their home.[26] He has all but forgotten the old days and is now occupied with problems of power distribution for the Dallas Light and Power Company. He is still the lean, dark boy with an analytic turn of mind, but the old thrill of life, with every day an unforeseen adventure, has left him and he is worrying about how he is going to buy a home.

Abie Faneuf

And there was Abie Faneuf of immortal memory, a great good-natured Yankee. It is a trick of the human mind, say psychologists, to seize upon that which is unique and unusual, rather than that which is commonplace and meritorious. This must be

---

26 Presumably, the visit occurred during Cy Corbett's "Pilgrimage" in 1923.

the explanation of Abie, for everyone I have talked to remembers him, even those who did not know him by name. And his uniqueness as a flyer cannot be overemphasized.

At a field where there were scores of extraordinarily good flyers, Abie played a role of comic fool. His flying was so rotten that it was a common saying that when Abie "took off" everyone else came down, and these boys were not given to great precautionary measures.

Abie's brand of flying was, like British statesmanship, a running series of compromises. Abie "flew the ship" part of the time, but most of the time it "flew him." To say a ship flew the pilot meant this: that, for the sake of averting immediate disaster, a pilot would change his mind about the maneuver he intended to execute and do that which appeared easier and safer. For instance, if he intended to do a 180-degree right turn and found that by turning into the wind, he was losing flying speed (and courage), he would change his mind after 45 degrees of the turn and continue straight ahead until he got up enough courage to try the turn again. This state of mind resulted in a ship's course which from the ground appeared very eccentric. And the funniest part about the whole thing was that Abie could not see anything unusual about his flying. He sincerely believed that the boys were ragging him when they would come around and touch his cot for luck, and ask him how much longer he intended to cheat the undertaker. Personally, I have never seen such luck as attended Abie. Up to July 1919, when he was honorably discharged with a commission at one of the Fort Worth fields, Abie's flying never changed a whit and he never had a bad crash. It was said that the Government gave Abie a commission, not for his flying, but for his luck. Then there was another saying, somewhat blasphemous, that the Second Person of the Trinity rode in the front seat when Abie flew.

If there was anyone to whom Abie was comparable as a flyer it was Captain Dodd, in charge of flying, a Kiwi ground officer who acquired wings by main force and determination.

Everyone gave Dodd a wide berth in the air, and would, if possible, manufacture engine or spark-plug trouble and land. But among the ground officers of his mess Dodd was not a little proud of his status as a flyer.

Many stories circulated about Abie and Dodd, too numerous to recount, but I will remember one that concerns them both. It was the day Abie soloed (first flew alone). It was a pleasant morning in May 1918 and Dodd was sitting in a motorcycle side car beside the "T," enjoying the spectacle before him. About a dozen planes were flying around the field, landing and taking off again. Abie showed promise in his dual work, so the instructor soloed him at about four-and-one-half hours. Abie came around for his first landing. He made a perfect three-point landing, but it was thirty-five feet in the air. The plane "pancaked," or sloshed down within a few feet of a smash when Abie "gave her the gun" and slid into the air (miraculously enough). This was the first manifestation of Abie's extraordinary luck. Abie came around a second, a third and a fourth time, repeating his first performance and never touching wheel to ground. Dodd convulsed with laughter, and among the cadets money was five to one that Abie couldn't come around again without cracking up. He did, and as the whole field was watching him, Abie did it a fifth, sixth, seventh and eighth time. The much-attempted landing Abie made about twenty-five feet in the air, directly over Dodd and his motorcycle. No one who saw it will ever forget with what celerity Dodd stopped laughing, left his motorcycle and betook himself out of harm's way. No one I have talked to seems to remember exactly how Abie landed that day, but the consensus is that the only permanent injury was suffered by Captain Dodd's dignity.

Abie Faneuf, flyer extraordinaire and supreme favorite of Lady Luck, is a chemist somewhere in the East, and had exchanged the stick and rudder for test tube and precipitates. Thus had another good soldier faded away.

Herrin

Every outfit had its professional soldier of fortune, and Herrin was ours. He was a silent, sleepy sort of man, slim and of sandy complexion. In his thirty-five years he had been everywhere and seen everything. He had fought with the British in northern India and on the Veldt. He had owned a silver mine in Mexico; to protect his interest he had become a machine gunner and helped to put down one of their many revolutions. In one of the other squadrons at Love he found another American who had been a machine gunner for the revolutionists, and who had fought against him at the siege of Mexico City. These two old soldiers would go off together for a holiday, and from the condition of their return, I surmise they spent most of their weekends toasting the siege of Mexico City.

Herrin was the most expert goldbricker I ever saw. He never obeyed an order; he never joined a detail and was never known to be present at a formation or roll call—except once—and that happened when the formation was called at a point which, by purest chance, happened to lie between where Herrin was and where he was going, on one of his silent, mysterious errands. He hove to around a corner of the barracks just as his name was called and answered *present* without changing his course or slowing his pace, or without a smile.

Nobody ever knew Herrin to attend class, nobody remembers flying with him, but I seem to vaguely recall seeing him take off in a ship one day. He must have flown enough to solo, for in time he got his wings and was commissioned.

It was during the cadet days that Captain Dodd issued a ridiculous order that the cadets would not sit down, lie down, or assume any other than an upright posture while waiting out around the "T" for their turn to fly.

It was during this period of stress that Herrin introduced his justly celebrated game, "The Potato Bug Race."

A circle was described (as geometricians say) on smooth, unvegetated ground, about three feet in diameter. Its center was "indicated" by slight depression. The cadets gathered round and so did the officer in charge of flying. As this officer could not recall, offhand, any army regulations, field rules or any of Captain Dodd's numerous bulletins prohibiting or regulating potato bug races, he let the game continue.

Any person desirous of entering a candidate retired a short distance and procured himself a potato bug (in which the country abounded) of superior breed and sporting blood. An ante or entrance fee of two bits was deposited with the treasurer; and side bets on any of the contestants were permissible. The six contestants were then deposited somewhere near the center of the circle and the race began.

The noise and enthusiasm engendered by the owners and spectators at this point in the race brought back the officer in charge of flying to make sure he was not being fooled by a disguised craps game.

For the benefit of those who are not close observers of potato bug life, let me remark here that this genus of insect exhibits a unique inconsistency of purpose in travel. Sometimes a bug would get to the very rim of the circle, its backers full of the virus of victory, and then would change its mind and amble back to its starting point and proceed to take a nap.

To cut the story short, Herrin's bug won the first three races and then one of the brighter cadets paid him one dollar for the winning bug. Herrin went off into the grass and got himself another bug which he entered in the next race and won again. After the second bug had won a few races another cadet purchased it for one dollar. Herrin got another bug and continued to win as before.

After Herrin was about fifteen dollars to the good, the entrants and spectators by common consent called off the race and asked him to explain. He did, as follows: a potato bug always seeks the shady side of a leaf. Herrin always managed to stand between his candidate and the sun, and with his hand keep the prospect of pleasant shade always before his bug!

But, like all old soldiers, Herrin too has "faded away"—only literally. After the Armistice he betook himself from the scene, on one of his silent, mysterious errands, to far-off lands, and nobody has heard of him since.

de Gozzaldi

There was de Gozzaldi whom I will always remember as a clever and courageous pilot. He was an Austrian by birth, an American by adoption (no man was ever a better American) and a graduate of Harvard. The boys called him "the Duke" because there was a story that his father was an exiled Austrian nobleman. About this story "the Duke" never ventured an opinion. He was well liked for his own good qualities.

When assigned to long cross-country jaunts, the "Duke," Bud Fisher and I would meet over White Rock (a large lake on the other side of Dallas) and fly formation and sometimes a little pseudo "combat" work over the tedious miles to Kaufman or Texarkana.

It might be well to remark here that cadets, in their anxiety to learn all about the game, were usually several stages ahead of where the official bulletins listed them. By that I mean that the Duke, Bud and I were doing combat work, although our well-meaning Uncle had us listed on the Cross-Country stage. The officer in charge of the stage evidently suspected what was going on, for he would send out the ships ten minutes apart.

On a beautiful morning in June that was big Fate for the Duke. He took off on Cross-Country for the town of Kaufman, after first ascertaining the number of the ship I was to fly. (These numbers were painted on the side of the fuselages large enough to be distinguishable at a distance in the air.) I was in my ship and ready to take off, ten minutes later, when the commander of the stage came up and requisitioned the ship. He turned it over to an officer I didn't recognize. After a meticulous examination of the control cables this officer got in and took off.

Now I knew that the Duke was waiting for me over White

Rock and also knew that he would recognize the ship by its number and think I was in it. But I felt assured that the chances that this officer would pass over White Rock were negligible.

An hour later I managed to get another ship and started on my belated trip to Kaufman. Passing over White Rock I kept a weather eye out for the Duke, for we had a new stunt in combat flying we were to practice that day. I didn't find him and thought no more about it until, upon returning to the field late that afternoon, I heard the big news.

It was a colonel of artillery who had taken my first ship that morning. He was little better than a solo bird and a rotten flyer at that. But he wanted the wings and so was bound to see the thing through.

As luck would have it, he passed over White Rock at the time I was due. The Duke, thinking it was I, dropped from a higher altitude and started the "combat work" in good earnest. With the accumulated speed of his descent he made a terrific pass at the colonel, zooming over his ship as he crossed it. Theoretically the Duke scored, after his surprise attack, and held up his arm in token of victory (for the colonel was supposed to be then "shot down"). As the Duke wheeled around to renew the combat, he noticed that the other ship had careened and fallen into a spin. Falling into a spin, or simulating death of the pilot, is a well-known stratagem in combat flying, and often enables the attacked to elude the attacker, especially when the latter had greater speed or skill. As his quarry spun down, the Duke pursued him in a sharp dive and when the colonel finally pulled up out of the spin the Duke was still "on his tail." From then on, the colonel flew an undeviating course and after several attacks from the sides and rear and from the front (for the Duke was a good pilot and by no means easy to shake off), the Duke began to suspect that something was amiss—the other plane showed so little enthusiasm for the game.

After due cogitation the Duke wheeled sharply and climbed away from the other ship.

When he landed later at Love Field the Duke was greeted by no less a person than the commandant himself and placed under arrest in the guardhouse, to be tried by a court martial.

The colonel, it seems, after his unfortunate encounter with the Duke, had managed to stagger back to the field in a fainting condition, and put his ship down without mishap. He remembered the number of the Duke's ship, and to say that he raised the devil with everybody in authority at Love does not state the case at all. In due time when the court martial was called he preferred charges against the Duke and did his best to "bust" him. The Duke was fined three months' pay and cautioned against premature "combat work," and the colonel flew no more at our field.

***

The Duke is still in Dallas. He is working as an advertising solicitor for the *Dallas News*. After the war he organized an oil company and promptly went broke. After that he had various economic adventures in the real estate business and as a traveling salesman for an electric light-fixture house. Last Sunday the Duke and I drove out to White Rock in his little roadster, to see a waterfront lot in a new real estate development which the Duke was thinking of buying.

As we stood there looking out over the waters of White Rock, he did not even remember the time he had chased the fierce but fainting artillery colonel out of the air to the very water's edge.

NINE

Texas Twilight

IT WAS THE LOVELY TEXAS TWILIGHT that got me. At the end of the day's flying two or three of us had been sent off, in different directions, to practice landings and get in flying time. We would fly around an imagined square, touch down and take off again before the machine stopped rolling. We had sharp instructions to be "home" before absolute dark. And to count our landings.

The weather was very calm. The engine was behaving perfectly. The beautiful little Curtiss 0X5 was powerful, reliable and quiet. It was new then, and we regarded it as the engineering triumph of the century. The machine seemed completely obedient to the man at the controls. The ship responded so beautifully it seemed that at last the air had become man's natural element.

The air upstairs was serene, very blue and seemed as tangible as water. The ship traveled in it with ease, and buoyantly, like a playful dolphin. The motions required for ascent, turn and descent became so automatic as to be almost unconscious. Everything induced in the pilot an out-of-this-world dreamy feeling, like Icarus. Or like the angels must feel when they are just hovering around, putting in time.

View of Love Field from the air, as seen by Cy Corbett, 1918.
(Courtesy of T.C. Corbett Family Archives)

The Texas nightfall was long and lingering. Time had virtually stopped. I thought of my mother back home, and of our little family—how she struggled to give us the best on an inadequate income. I thought of my brother and his pet dog Spot, an intelligent mutt that was almost human. I thought of Sis Walsh, part of my heart and a lovely sea-gamine walking out of the waves at old South Haven. Since we had read the *Eclogues* in school I always thought of her as the nymph Galatea. *Galatea in Michigan*, the title of a book I would write someday. Some Roman artist had done a fresco for a rich senator's villa, "Venus Arising from the Sea." The picture had vanished centuries ago but its reputation survived. *Galatea in Michigan* would be a greater work—if I lived.

Then I thought of the brilliant men at school (St. Ignatius), behind the old grey walls already fifty years old. They would go on for year after year, after I was dead, giving the dirt-poor young Irish a brief taste of learning. Bakewell, Garvy, how attractive their lives of study seemed.

I came down so hard I was afraid I had cracked something. It jerked me out of a reverie and I realized with a shock that I couldn't see the ground. I had been feeling for the ground. The tactic was, hand on throttle, to slow down and hold her in a slight stall a few feet off the ground. She could pancake as much as seven feet without damage. But this last bump, I realized, was too much. And now I couldn't risk another takeoff.

I taxied slowly and carefully until I found a farmer's set of buildings. I went in and phoned the field. They sent a small truck with three men to rope down the plane and to take me home.

It was just supper, back in the noisy barracks. The two Bud Fishers and Bob Wemban got a big laugh out of my plight, with much ribald joshing until I thought I might really be in trouble with the front office—which in this case was not the field commandant but the engineering subdivision in charge of maintenance.

The next day the young colonel in charge, Col. Cunningham, merely smiled as I tried to explain what happened. How the lovely Texas twilight sort of mesmerized me. But I quickly added that I didn't crack anything. His good-natured understanding made me think he must have had a similar experience.

He was a bright young engineer-designer, with the wings, who had been a professor at M.I.T. He was on a tour of duty to get some experience with the squadrons. Those Easterners from the big colleges were quiet types but very bright. I pegged him for the new intellectual—one who deals in science and atomic research. I can still see his odd smile. I think he understood. He merely said, "You were very lucky."

Years later there dawned on me the proper classification of my odd experience. It was the same tale of enchantment that Ulysses told, and was badly believed. It was my Song of the Sirens—only with aerial trimmings. The more things change, the more they are the same, as somebody said.

***

Fr. Furay and My A.B.

While in Texas deeply engrossed in learning to fly, I got a distressed letter from Mother. She said my class had graduated with no mention of my name anywhere. I wrote to Fr. Furay, remote and inaccessible president of the University, reminding him of his promise that if Harvard and Yale were granting degrees (to the boys not finishing because of their service), Ignatius would too.

He said the situation had changed and he couldn't do it unless I would return to take and pass all the final examinations.

So, I spent a day at the old college. Five of seven professors whose classes I had taken waved me on and signed the paper. Two of the examinations I took, and squeezed thru, thanks to the kindly teachers, I must say. Furay had the sheepskin ready and presented it to me in his office the next day. He did not seem to be too happy about it. But it was nevertheless a genuine St. Ignatius A.B., all wool and a yard wide. I valued it but never found any use for it. (It finally burned up in my Army locker, in a fire we had on this place in 1963.) *Sic transit gloria mundi*.

If I could only have realized at the time how much more valuable to me than the degree were the contacts I made with learned teachers, and boys who were to be lifelong friends.

Editor's Note: The men at St. Ignatius were very influential and largely shaped the way Thomas Cyril Corbett viewed life. Many of his mentors and classmates remained in contact with him throughout his life, and helped shape his philosophy. In later years Cy attended the annual reunions of the classes of 1916–18, finally abandoning the pilgrimages when only three alumni were healthy enough or had the energy to show up.

St. Ignatius class of 1918, with identification of individuals handwritten by T.C. Corbett.
(Courtesy of T.C. Corbett Family Archives)

Editor's Note: Following the trip to Chicago to straighten out the matter of receiving his college degree, Cy began a "flight diary." Dorothy Lyons, Cy's one-time girlfriend, had given him a small, leather-bound *Soldier's Diary* in which to keep notes about his life in the Army Air Corps. Below are various entries from that diary.

1918 Flight Diary

July 28, 1918, Sunday
Last Friday I left Chicago to return to Love Field, my furlough being up. The train journey was a melancholy affair, and my heart was heavy for saying good-bye to the ones I love. But this morning the sun was shining, and I hear once more the voice of multifarious adventure.

July 29, 1918, Monday

The planes are buzzing around and I go out to fly at 9 o'clock for the first time in 25 days. Wonder if I still know how. Will soon find out. Anyway, couldn't sleep for hours last night. It was very hot.

Cross-Country trip to Waxahachie today. While searching the ground for the right railroad, nearly went into a spin. Engine got very hot (190 degrees) several times. Had to throttle down and glide to cool off. Found Waxahachie.

Hit a hard bump taking off for home and thought I had cracked the landing gear, but could not see on account of large blind angle on a Curtiss. Hit several wicked air bumps on way home. Landed tail very low, in case the landing gear might have been wiped off. But it was there. I was so intent on a tail-low landing I didn't notice that she zoomed before losing flying speed. Hit with an awful wallop. Thanks to good construction, everything held. Hot as Hell. Going to bathe and then to the cadet club. There is a rumor that our pay had been cut to $30.00 a month.

July 30, 1918, Tuesday

Williamson of the 136th Squadron and I walked down to the N.C.O. Club last night and talked till late. I was very homesick and sick from the heat and too much pop. Got up this morning with a headache and nauseated. After a two-hour wait on the field, got a ship. The Cross-Country trips were to McKinney, a good-sized town about thirty-five or forty miles north of here. I was just about all in when I started and shouldn't have taken the chance, only I wanted very much to finish the Cross-Country.

Took off and flew northeast, in the direction of White Rock, until I picked up the second railroad, as per directions. Followed it through Richardson, a small town, recognized by the little white church at the end of the business street. On to Plano, easily recognized by its name painted on the roof of a factory, for the special benefit of flyers.

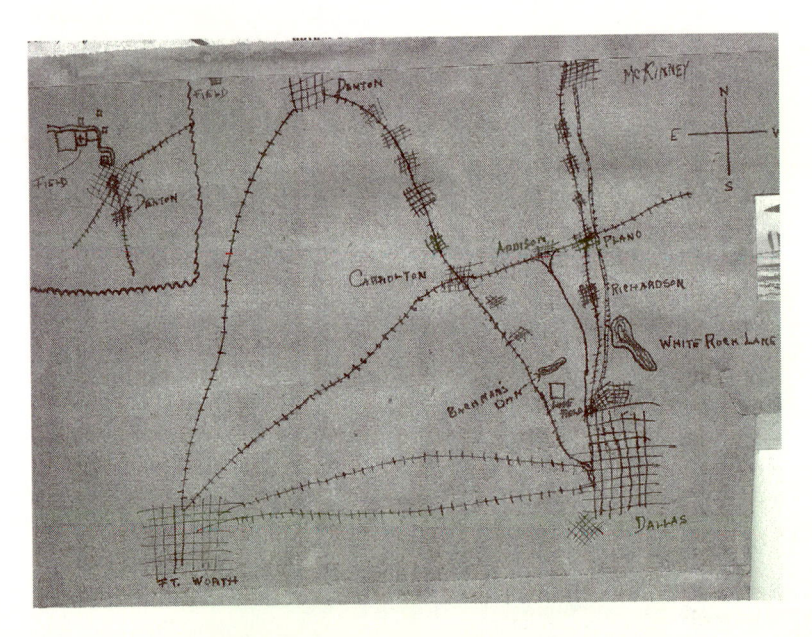

Cy Corbett's hand-drawn flight map, showing his cross-country journey of July 30, 1918.
(Courtesy of T.C. Corbett Family Archives)

After I left Plano, I closed the throttle nearly all the way and stalled along as I didn't want to get there too quickly. I needed two hours and forty minutes. Lost altitude rapidly, coming down from 3,400 to 1,800 too fast. It made me very sick. Things began to get dark and I had a sharp pain in the pit of my stomach. Remembered that if I came down and landed, I would have some explaining to do. Would have to take the physical examinations all over again and risk a discharge. The chances are that a man will come to with a sudden loss of altitude. So I "kept on carrying on" and pretty soon felt a little better.

Soon came to the town of Allen. A few miles out of Allen I discovered that a long strip of aluminum sheeting on the cowl was hanging loose. The air pressure was bending it back and I saw that it would soon break off. I remembered an incident I heard told of two flyers who were up scattering handbills for a celebration of some kind. A bunch of them slipped from the hand of one of the men and flew back and broke two stabilizer wires.

Decided that I had better come down and fix it. Closed the throttle and glided down looking for a good field. I saw a fair one, and came down to a hundred feet, flew directly over it and looked it over carefully. It seemed all right but just a little small. I decided to circle back again and land on it. But on the first turn I saw a larger one below me. It was slightly rolling, but I thought its size compensated for that. I got a good distance to the leeward of it and glided in. While I was still rolling fast the

Landing in a farmer's field was not uncommon when flying the JN-4D cross country.
(Courtesy of T.C. Corbett Family Archives)

machine hit a small hollow which tipped it so hard on one wing as nearly to break a wing skid. But they were steel and held. If they were the old Standard's bamboo they would have cracked. Came to a stop, cut off the engine and got out. No tires blown. Everything O.K. *Deo gratiae.*

    I pulled the torn strip of metal off and threw it away. Went off to look over the field to see which way I would take off. Before I got to the end, a man in an auto drove in. I asked him where I could get a drink of water. He told me to hop in his car. His family got out to look at the plane and I told his little girl that she was in charge of it (Field Regulation #9729). He drove me across the field to a well. I had a cold drink and immediately felt better. Texas heat is the devil.

    When we got back there were about a dozen cars and a lot of people around the ship. I got a kid to sit in it and hold back the stick while I cranked it. I taxied into position, cut the switch and got out and looked the field over again. I first decided to take off cross-wind as in any other position the field was very bumpy. I threw some Texas dirt high in the air and decided that the wind was too strong. Searched the field in the wind direction and found a narrow strip that was fairly level. Asked some farmers to help me turn the machine around. The kid got in again and I cranked. Told the man who drove me to the well to be sure to pull me out before the ship burned, if I should crash. This was my feeble attempt at witticism, but he evidently mistook it and the look of horror on his face I will not soon forget. Had two men on each wing holding back the machine while I opened the throttle.

    When I raised my arm to let go, the machine shot forward, gathered speed and hopped a few hollows. I pulled it up but didn't have enough speed. It settled down and touched gently. I pushed the stick forward and eased it back. She lifted off the ground and I cleared some trees beyond the field by a good margin. Banked around, flew over the little crowd and waved my arm at them in token of farewell. They waved back. Then struck off in a northern direction. Soon was over McKinney and turned northwest. After about three minutes I noticed the field under me. There were several machines at one end of it and along the road a line of automobiles. Glided in, landed and taxied to the line. Pretty sick when I got out, so folded up my helmet, put it under my head and stretched out under a ship.

Biplane fueling at Love Field.
(Courtesy of University of North Texas Libraries, "The Portal to Texas History," Dallas Municipal Archives)

A lieutenant came along and told me to get up and help gas the ships. I did, thinking a few uncomplimentary things. Helped around a little, cranked a prop and went over to a farmhouse where I got a glass of milk. Offered to pay for it but the lady refused, saying she wouldn't take money from a soldier. It was a good thing, because when I looked for some, I discovered I didn't have any! Came back, gassed my ship and while I was helping another fellow, some of the boys came along with a box of sandwiches. I tried to eat but couldn't. One fellow had a can of beer. I drank some but it didn't mix well with the milk. Started back and got home without any further adventure, but still a little shaky. When I finally touched ground at Love Field again I was profoundly grateful, for I had taken a big chance and gotten away with it.

The boys in the barracks have been singing all the old songs tonight. Temperature 109 degrees; time today 2:45 hours. If the brass hats have made no mistake in keeping my time, my Cross-Country should now be complete.

August 1, 1918, Thursday

Yesterday I went to the training office and reminded them that I had finished my Cross-Country time. They transferred me to Formation. Went out on field at 6 a.m. and stayed till 9. Did not get to fly as there were too many ahead of me. But sat around dreaming of my commission.

When we came into the barracks we were put on detail to bail out a cellar. Thus do our dreams of glory come to dust. The detail didn't show up so another fellow and I did it.

August 2, 1918, Friday

No chance to fly today. There are now 46 in Formation of which I am about the 26th.

There was an accident here today. Details are very vague. It said that one of our planes caught fire at 3,000 feet (from backfire). One man jumped out at 500 feet. The other burned to death. Another version of the rumor said there was only one man in the plane and he burned up. The victims were 2nd lieutenants stationed around here, whom I did not know.[27] Ominous

---

27 According to the *Corsicana Daily Sun* of Aug. 2, 1918, Lt. Robinson E. Bridwell of West Bluff, California, was killed when he jumped from an altitude of five hundred feet to escape flames from his burning plane. The incident occurred about nine miles south of Dallas.

sight—saw board officers going to take an inventory of the deceased's effects.

August 3, 1918, Saturday

This is written just as the dawn is breaking. A score of ships are buzzing on the line and another score are taking off. It is a beautiful sight. The east is crimson and the Morning Star is still shining faintly. Motorcycle sidecars are racing up and down the line. Officers in charge are giving final orders and the ships—in twos and threes—are racing from the line into the wind. Their tails lift off the ground, they gather speed and then lift gently. Sometimes they touch again for one last farewell to Mother Earth and then they zoom up, much as a man leaving something he loves.

Above, the eastern light is creeping across the sky, changing it to azure—and ships, singly or in formations of three and four, dot the sky. To fly is wonderful. These leviathans of the air are the winged monsters of another era that is now just dawning.

August 4, 1918, Sunday Night

Am writing this by arc-light which is shining in through my window. Saturday went downtown and polished the silver wings, which I have long kept in anticipation of the happy day.

August 5, 1918, Monday

Did not fly. Still stalled in Formation. But we all received ground instruction in echelon flying—and then raked up the cadet grounds. Temp. 100 degrees in the shade.

August 6, 1918, Tuesday

For the first time flew Formation today with Lt. Rainey, an old friend of mine. We were in the leading ship. Formation is interesting work so long as the other fellow doesn't clip your flippers off. We covered about 60 miles. Flew near McKinney and to the other side of White Rock. It certainly is a strange sight to see the other ships rising or falling back or catching up. We are unused to seeing things up there. I like Formation.

Went up to see Sgt. Maj. Williams of the 136th and walked to the gate with him as he was going to town. His sister is in from Claybourne, Texas. After he was gone I stayed at the gate talking to the guard and a plane droned overhead. It was Major Netherwood's big Hispano-Curtiss, a beauty—and the best ship on this field. Suddenly the engine stopped dead and the silence was painful. The plane was about 500 feet up and a little north of the gate. It was a case of dead stick. The guard immediately lifted the receiver of his phone and called the hospital for an ambulance. Instead of gliding back to the field, which he had lots of room to do, Netherwood went straight ahead and landed down behind the machine gun range, near the lake, in a little clearing on very uneven ground. I ran a couple of blocks to where he crashed. The ship was badly washed-out but neither the Major nor his mechanic was hurt. He would never have smashed if he turned and glided to the field. A lot of flyers say the same thing. Which only goes to show that even Majors sometimes make mistakes! That same Major has punished a great many cadets for pulling less bonehead stunts.

Then to the Y where a strange officer sang "They are Hanging Danny Deaver" and "Mandalay." He made an awful hit. Strange how the men like Kipling.

August 8, 1918, Thursday

Yesterday I flew V Formation, right-hand side. Time 65 minutes. Came in and played two sets of tennis on our new court. I played with Peterson, a Harvard man. Though Harvard men are supposed to do all things well, Petey couldn't save the game, and we were nicely trimmed.

Today flew five-ship echelon Formation. Place: 2nd. Flew 50 feet behind the 1st ship and of all the thrills in my life some moments up there were the greatest. Nearly ran into the pilot ship once. Held the ship up and stalled it while he got out from under. Weather very bumpy. The Lieutenant in charge said that we flew too close for this weather. Fourth ship, Sammy, who beat us at tennis yesterday, was wilder than a March hare. He overshot third ship repeatedly. Expected to see Stall come down without any flippers. Once I ducked my head inside the cockpit to listen to the engine, which sounded as though it was backfiring. When I looked out, I was nearly on the 1st ship's back. Highest Altitude 4,800.

After we were down about 1½ hours we were let go up again. My ship (42) refused to start and the others went without me. Lt. Russell came over just before they got it started and said he wanted it to hunt some birds who were down on forced landing. Asked him if I could ride with him. He said yes, if I wanted to ride in the front seat. (He evidently doesn't think much of his own flying.) I said "sure" and got in, as I figured that one risk more or less doesn't amount to much in this game. We soon spotted the forced landing and then my Formation. We wheeled around and got in third place. Clouds about 2,500 feet. We flew through several and nearly lost the other ships, though they weren't more than 150 feet away. We left them after a while and Russell stunted down through the clouds—a very risky business, as in clouds you can't see even your own wing tips. When we got down, he asked me not to mention the stunting. It is strictly forbidden on a crowded field, near clouds, or with any but a stunt ship. He was out of order on three counts, so I recognized the psychological moment to ask him if I couldn't count some of the joy ride as Formation time. He said, "Yes, count it all." I now have 3:45 hours of the seven required. I would have been out of luck for graduating with my class if I had not gone with Russell. As it is, I will finish Saturday.

August 9, 1918, Friday

Last evening I went swimming at the Country Club with the people I met there last Saturday. There is a little lagoon at the bottom of a natural ravine which is all fixed up after the manner of country clubs. It is a very pretty spot. The daughter of the family is quite a swimmer and I was winded with trying to keep up with her. As B.L.T.[28] would say, "All Horrors of War." After swimming we played nine holes on the putting course which is electric lighted.

When I arrived back at the Field there was a little package on my bed. It was after "Taps" and every light was out, but I was consumed with curiosity to know what it contained. It was a soldier's copy of *Science and Health*, which Sis Walsh very kindly sent. It was well met; for in this game you need a good deal of science to keep your health. Printed on India paper and bound in sheepskin, it is as neat a piece of typography as I have ever seen.

Flew Formation this morning for 75 minutes. Total time now 5:07. Ought to finish Monday. Flew fourth place. We had a good formation. Nothing eventful, except Stoll had a slow ship

Planes in formation.
(Courtesy of T.C. Corbett Family Archives)

---

28 B.L.T. was Bert Leston Taylor, who was the "conductor" (editor) of the *Tribune's* "Line 'O Type or Two" column.

in 3rd place and I had to do considerable waiting for him. Nearly stalled a couple of times. Bayer was in 5th place and while I was waiting for Stoll he had to wait for me. He went off in a tailspin but soon pulled out again and climbed into position. A crosscurrent caught him and drifted him athwart my path of flight and dangerously close to the tail of my ship.

He wheeled around, bucked the wind, climbed for altitude and then dove into place. Half turned in the seat, I watched him out of the corner of my eye. While he was diving at me, I had all the sensation that must occur when a little German Albatross or Fokker is diving from above and behind you with its machine gun spitting. It was one of the few great moments that are vouchsafed to any man. Second ship set distance of about 150 feet this morning. Highest Altitude 3,800 feet. Order: (1) Farley (2) Sam (3) Stoll (4) Corbett (5) Bayer.

August 10, 1918, Saturday

Flew three formations of 60, 65, and 35 minutes, and now I am finished with flying. The last trip kept me thinking of the first trip I made, March 15th, with old Foote. I thought then it was wonderful beyond words, and also that I would never be able to fly alone. But now that it is over, primary flying seems the easiest thing in the world.

The first trip this morning was with Lieutenant Buck Hefron. If a wilder man than Abie Faneuf ever left the ground, it is he. After the formation closed in at 1,000 feet he cut the throttle almost entirely and stuck the nose up at what felt to be about 45 degrees, waiting for the 2nd ship to fly closer. But it didn't, so we stalled along that way for about three miles and the ship settled up to 400 feet. I had to keep kicking the rudder all the way over to keep the ship from going into a spin. We started to spin once, but I caught it in the first whip and managed to climb back quickly into place in the formation. If we had gone into a first-rate spin there was hardly altitude enough to pull out before crashing. I had visions of another Maloney-Ghee incident.

Hefron would have been killed in the front seat. I would have escaped, undoubtedly, but I didn't like the idea of having to fish Buck out of wreckage. After about 20 minutes, when he saw that the second ship wouldn't close in, he opened up the throttle to about 1100 revs. and we picked up altitude to 1500 feet where I drew a long breath. When we came down, he said, "Corbett, you're a damn good flyer." But Hefron not only is a good flyer, he doesn't know what fear is. He is what they call a "flying fool."

The second trip I made in "40." That ship was like a 1908 Ford—in the last stages of decrepitude, and I knew it as soon as I got into the air. The engine missed and she wouldn't climb. The formation was soon 500 feet above me and a mile ahead. However, I followed along and by cutting several corners I finally caught them and fell into fifth place. Every time the ship rode a bump, a spray of water or gas would hit me in the face. That suggested that the mechanic had left the cap off the gas tank. Tried to see it by leaning out but couldn't. I decided then that it was about "50–50" to burn up or fall out. So I unfastened my belt, waited for a calm area, and let go the rudder; steadying the stick with the fingers of my left hand, I stood up, and to my satisfaction saw that the cap was on. You probably wonder why a little thing like the gas tank cap should worry me three thousand feet up. It is just such little things that count in the game where "eternal vigilance is the price of—" life.

When I came down, I was lucky enough to get a ship again—went up in third place. Flew around Oak Cliff and Highland Park and spotted the Country Club from the air. Didn't have any difficulty, because I had "46," a good fast ship. I noticed that the 5th ship kept a good distance back. It was Sammy. When he came down and was asked by someone what his trouble was, he said that he had gone all through the course without breaking his neck and he wasn't taking any chances on his last ride!

Am now finished with flying and ought to get the commission about Tuesday or Wednesday.

August 11, 1918, Sunday
Out to dinner with Williamson, Davis, Marty, and Strington. Ran the guard.

August 12, 1918, Monday
In an auto accident tonight. Today spent getting class releases signed up—paper had to be signed by fourteen officers.

August 13, 1918, Wednesday
Signed the oath and a lot of other papers. Had to swear that my crash was not on purpose! Turned in issued clothing to Q.M. and am, as I write this, waiting to go to Adjutants office to take the final oath. This is the day of days when dreams come true.

Lt. T.C. Corbett wearing his newly acquired wings.
(Courtesy of T.C. Corbett Family Archives)

Conclusion
(Written on the train returning to Chicago,
Friday, August 16, 1918)

After much waiting Wednesday, we were finally called into the Adjutants office about 4 p.m. We signed several more papers, including a discharge as a private, and our acceptance of commission.

There is more red tape in this than in anything I ever heard of. Then we went into the inner sanctum and the Adjutant asked if there were any Germans or Austrians in the crowd. Then he asked for those whose parents were of alien birth. Petey's were born in Denmark, Sam's in Germany, also Stoll's; de Gozzaldi admitted that his father had been a general in the Austrian army. O'Brien's and McClellan's were born in Ireland, which caused a laugh all around. Then we all held up our right hands and swore to support the constitution of the United States and to execute the duties of our office to the best of our ability.

It gave me a mighty thrill to think that Washington and his officers had taken this same oath. Then the Adjutant told us that we were now lieutenants, to put on the gold bars. And he congratulated us. We were given temporary papers certifying to our commission. Mine said,

"You, Thomas Cyril Corbett, are hereby notified that the President of the United States has appointed you Second Lieutenant A.S., M.A., R.A., R.M.A." All of which means Air Service, Military Aeronautics, Regular Army, Reserve Military Aviator.

To realize my ambition, at last to have the privilege of wearing the badge of an honorable service, this was a feeling that shook me down to my heels. It was worth going through all the gaff for. And that is saying much. Beyond this words do not go.

Thursday morning I flew with that fastidious Frenchman, Requa. He is a marvelous flyer. We did contact work (low flying), and he did some hair-raising vertical banks around haystacks, about ten or fifteen feet off the ground. In an earlier trip we flew twenty-five feet over a railroad train and dove down across its path, only a little ahead of the engine.

Thursday night Country Club again.

Friday, I flew three hours practicing solo contact work.

I landed in a stubble wheat field in which a little kid of 13 was plowing. He ran a half mile across the rough ground in his bare feet to find the time for me. I was struck by his unselfishness and gave him one of my gold collar bars. I had no money. He had a very intelligent face.

While I was on the ground yesterday, between rides, Harrison said he had acquired a ship and asked me to go for a joyride with him. I said I would be glad to. "Wait till I get my goggles." But the fellow I had lent them to was gone. I would have gone without them but I have a superstition against doing this. Though I went through the whole barracks asking for a pair, I couldn't get any, as they were all in use or closely held. So I couldn't go. Harrison then asked Emerie, who went. They got tangled up in a high-tension electric line and both are in the hospital as I write this. Someone said that one broke a leg and the other an arm, and both were badly bruised. We went to the hospital last night but the orderly said that if we wanted any information we would have to come and see Major about it in the morning, which sounds bad. To bed. Harrison had his leave, and was all ready to go home.

This morning as I was climbing into a ship for a Cross-Country triangle to Kaufman, Terrell and Love, a mechanic asked if I would like to take him along. I did. Over the edge of White Rock I had a rendezvous with de Gozzaldi and De Learie. I looked long and hard for them and finally spotted one far below. Cut the motor and spiraled and "S'ed" down and fell in behind them in formation. Two more joined us and we flew V and Echelon formations half the way to Kaufman and then the fellows got tired and broke up, as Formation is hard work.

But we still kept in sight. Did sort of a slipless falling leaf down into the Kaufman field, reported and took off again. Landed at Torrell, spent some little time on the ground and on the way back climbed steadily to 7,200 feet where cold kept me shivering as I had on only a silk shirt and light breeches. Highest Altitude reached directly over White Rock. When ceiling was reached, cut the throttle, dove, spiraled, vertical—banked and spun down to 1,500 and landed a few minutes later at the field. The mechanic was ecstatic and somewhat dazed when he got out, and thanked me warmly. It is very funny to hear these older men calling me "Lieutenant." (Time 3:15.)

When I came in I found the leave I applied for yesterday was approved.

Had to write several military letters, fill out a pay voucher, and fix up final discharge, etc. Packed, dressed and left for the train inside an hour's time. And now—here I am on my way back to Chicago.

***

September 11, 1918, Wednesday

Am back at Love again after seven glorious days at home. At present am in Squadron #10, the unassigned squadron. We don't do any flying. Go to four classes a day. Gunnery 7:45, Radio 9:30, Navigation 10:30, and Engines 2:30. At 4:45 we have calisthenics or a hike. And then we go to town, passes good until 12 o'clock.

Lt. Suter, who was in our party Tuesday eve, crashed today and broke his leg. Poor old Petey, with whom I was commissioned, my tennis partner, was killed yesterday.

Am reading a book, the first I have since joining the army. That is, I am reading it when not interrupted by this lively gang who bunk around me—Dunnavan, de Gozzaldi, Stoll, R.H. O'Brien, Marty, and Wenban.

September 13, 1918, Friday

Two of our men were burned yesterday.[29] They were on their back, the rumor says, and couldn't turn over. Not sufficient altitude. They neglected to cut the switch when they crashed, so they burned up. Otherwise the one in the back seat might have been saved.

September 14, 1918, Saturday

Yesterday afternoon we all went to town in the post automobiles and marched from the undertaker's place to the station. There were two gray hearses with a single line of flying officers on each side as an escort, and behind the hearses there were about 100 more lieutenants in column formation. The band led the procession and played slow funeral music. As we marched, I could see that women standing on the sidewalks were crying, and one old man, probably an old soldier, came to salute as the hearse passed him. It was very solemn and very touching. The band played Chopin's "Marche Funebre," the sublimest music ever written, I do believe, and I could hardly repress the tears. When we came to the station the band lined up on one side of the hollow square and we in company front on the other. They took the caskets out of the hearse, and the pallbearers (all flying officers) bore them a-down our line and we came to a salute.

When the bodies came to the end of the little square, a bugler sounded "Taps." I could not stop the tears for those poor boys who would not fly again.

Tonight Lt. Williams and I attended "Fite Night" at Camp Dick. There were several good bouts and a knockout. All combinations from the military.

---

29   Lieutenant Parker Bruce of Chicago, Illinois, instructor, and Lt. Anthony A. Sego, student from Kentland, Indiana, were killed when their airplane fell several hundred feet about two miles north of Love Field. (*The Eagle*, Bryan, Texas, Sept. 13, 1918)

Funeral procession for unidentified military aviator at the Second Provisional Wing of the Air Service in Park Place, Texas.
(Source: Overseas Dreams, *1919, Press of Gulfport Printing, Houston, TX, pp. 148. DeGolyer Library, Southern Methodist University.)*

September 18, 1918, Wednesday
Last night at the Country Club and went swimming. Nearly froze. But afterwards drank hot coffee and prevented a heavy cold with aspirin.

September 20, 1918, Friday.
Two more of our men[30] were killed near Fort Worth yesterday. Both accidents resulted from a straight nosedive, as though the horizontal controls were snapped. We marched in the funerals today. They played the divine Chopin again. Some people

---

30   Second Lt. James L. McKeever, of New York City, and John M. Widenham, of Los Angeles, California, when their airplane went into a slide and crashed, about twenty miles north of Fort Worth, Texas. (*El Paso Herald*, Sept. 19, 1918)

say that there is no thought in music, but to me that music came with infinite tenderness and compassion—the articulate voice of love, transcending all words.

~1970 Recollection:

And here, with the slow tread of soldiers, and muffled drums and sorrowing fifes my little dog-eared diary ends abruptly. I have tried to remember why, and I cannot. It may have been because I had filled the little leather-bound book that Dorothy had given me. It may have been because our advanced course in flying became too arduous, and it may have been only the damnable Texas heat which soaked into your bones and lodges in your soul till it destroyed all capacity for action. But I am inclined to think that the reason why this diary ends where it does is my assignment to edit the eight-page base newspaper, *Love Field Loops*.

TEN

Army Journalism

Love Field Loops:

Somewhere back in about the middle of the summer, Major O'Connell (the "Irishman"), who was executive officer at the field, had decided to inaugurate a field newspaper. After the usual travail that attends the borning of such things, *Love Field Loops* was finally launched and became an eight-page newspaper containing news, opinion and advertising. It appeared, with more or less regularity, once a week, on Saturday. But to his grief the Irishman learned that the founding of a newspaper was about the easiest thing that attaches to it. His difficulty, beside the usual one with printers which is always to be expected, was with his editorial personnel. Newspaper men were scarce to begin with. And those who did have the experience would, in the manner of armies, never acknowledge it. No sooner would O'Connell get hold of a few good men than they would be graduated and sent overseas, or sent to another field.

So desperate did his plight become that some of the many orders, and memoranda from headquarters that were tacked up on the bulletin board, lost their mandatory tone and took on an attitude that was almost one of pleading. Instead of the usual notice "Flying cadets of both squadrons at the Field will henceforth etc., etc.," they became "Major O'Connell will regard it as a personal favor to him for any cadets having previous newspaper experience to assist in the publishing of the *Love Field Loops*." He also let it be "noised about" that he intended to do something handsome for the volunteers.

Still I can remember an extremely warm afternoon, early in September, when Duke de Gozzaldi and I were lying on adjoining bunks in the barracks (doing "bunk fatigue"). It was devilish hot and not possible to forget it. And although the daily hops we took about the countryside could never be said to be monotonous, still flying had lost for us its old kick. The Duke, with something akin to inspiration in his thin, ascetic face, suggested that we "get us a couple of jobs on the so-called *Love Field Loops*."

"Excellent idea," I said. So we did.

The Duke had written things for the *Harvard Lampoon*; after that, articles on music for one of the New York newspapers. My own experience had been confined to the *Loyola University Magazine*.

The editorial offices of the *Loops* was a small room in one end of the Y.M.C.A. shack. We had two typewriters, a journal and a day book, three wooden benches, chairs, a ream of yellow notepaper and a half-dozen pencils. A roll of wrapping paper had been requisitioned from somewhere. Its function was to determine the paper's format every Wednesday evening— though how the make-up editor ever managed was a triumph of quiet patience and determination.

Fully one quarter of that small room was totally lost to any purposes of journalism. It was stacked halfway to the ceiling with back numbers of the *Loops*. In spite of these apparent handicaps, stories were assigned and written in this room; material was assembled and the paper made up here and sent to a job printer in town. Proofs were read and corrected here, and here it was that the studious figure of John Dewey, the managing editor, performed the weekly miracle of getting out a paper on nothing at all.

Duke and I started in on the easy job of assignment reporters. We interviewed various celebrities about the field; we ran down rumors about anything from a proposed cut in pay to the wearing of Sam Brown belts by cadets. Our connection with the *Loops* lasted from about September 1st to November 1st, when we were sent to Roosevelt Field, Long Island, to join a squadron assembling there for service overseas.

Love Field: Y.M.C.A., 1918, where the camp newspaper *Love Field Loops* was housed.
(Courtesy of University of North Texas Libraries, "The Portal to Texas History," Dallas Municipal Archives)

It was, I think, because there is a greater kick in seeing your words in print, that the funny green scrawl in the *Soldier's Diary* became intermittent, and finally stopped altogether. It was not because of any dearth of material.

Editor's Note: In Cy Corbett's miscellaneous papers, a clipping of the *Love Field Loops* masthead was found, describing itself as "Issued Weekly by the Men of Love Field, Texas." Editor: Lt. J.P. Dewey, R.M.A.; Associate Editors: Lt. T.C. Corbett, R.M.A. and Lt. Lloyd Lehrbos, R.M.A. A nearly complete issue was also found containing the same information. It was Volume 1, Number 15, dated Oct. 12, 1918.

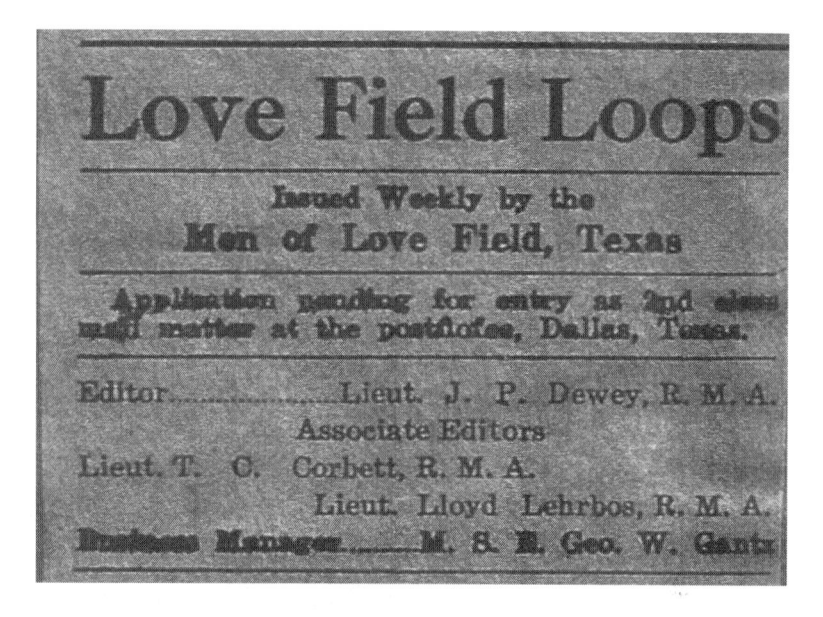

Masthead of *Love Field Loops*.

Editor John Dewey was a great, pleasant fellow who at 23 had worked on two or three small newspapers. He came to my bunk late one afternoon and said he had heard I was a bit of a writer, and he had a proposition for me.

Our commanding officer, a Kiwi colonel by the name of Dodd, a rough-spoken Irishman, had come up from the ranks, had been in the Philippines and, some said, the Boxer rebellion. The sharp necessity for officers had boosted him to his present rank, but he was still a diamond in the rough. Dewey had gone to him and offered to edit the camp newspaper if Dodd, in return, would jump him one hundred files ahead in the tedious waiting to be assigned overseas. There were not enough planes overseas and 4,000 young RMAs were cluttering American fields, just waiting. Dodd had agreed. Dewey would be the editor and he needed an assistant. He figured it would be only a month or two till he got the orders which would release him from the logjam of pilots.

Did I want the job? I did, if I could handle it, I told him. I had written a few pieces for him, but aside from that knew practically nothing about newspapering. He said that was good enough, that I was on.

Dewey had made a deal with a job printer in downtown Dallas, and Dodd assigned us a motorcycle and a sidecar with a driver and the right to use it any time of day or night.

The paper we printed on was not the best. The half-tones were smudgy and the contents seemed dull but nobody complained. Dewey was a good newspaperman for one so young. He had a sharp eye for trouble and managed to keep it out of the paper. We put notices on the bulletin boards requesting news items but most of them Dewey turned down because they were largely frivolous, ribald, or somebody's idea of a joke on a friend.

We divided the lead stories and interviews, and he carefully read my copy, introducing me to the ground rules. He was a wonderful realist and he kept a wonderful school. It was the way most great editors of the past had learned their trade.

I learned from Dewey that basic difficulty of newspaper writing—that you can't tell things as they really are, with exact truth. For, readers don't want to hear it that way. They would be mortally offended to realize the stinkyness of their own motive, and of human motives in general. So, newspaper writing is necessarily a mixture of as much sordid truth as you dare, and an idealized picture of the man as he would like to see himself, but isn't. That is newspaper writing, a screwy business, one that Freud should have explained.

Often I rode in to the printer with a last batch of copy. On the way back this particular day, I thought to stop at Camp Dick to see an old school friend, Leo McGivena, upperclassman, whom I had heard was there. The driver pulled up in front of the barracks and I went in looking for him. He was limp on his cot, just getting over the flu.[31]

I urged him to come for a little ride in the sidecar, as I thought it would do him a world of good. He reluctantly consented, and the driver and I helped him out and into the contraption. I told the driver to wait right there for us, that I would drive the machine he surrendered with some hesitation.

I climbed on and started it without trouble. I had run one once, but it was an Indian and this was a very powerful Harley-Davidson. The thing got underway with an awful jerk. I twisted the handles right and left until I thot I understood the speed control.

All this time we were going a little faster than we should, and erratically, thru the narrow streets of Camp Dick. We made a 180-degree curve and suddenly confronting us was a company front of men, from curb to curb. And, furthermore, they were a brass band, tooting away in the usual dismal army consonances.

I must have gotten rattled and twisted the throttle control the wrong way. For instead of slowing down, the machine leapt forward in a sickening way. I could see myself standing court-martial for mass murder.

You won't believe this, and I scarcely don't myself at this late date, but a lane opened up before us. We dashed thru it. Nobody got killed. Nobody got hurt. The band never missed a toot. I recovered control. The driver and I practically carried McGivena, now speechless, back to his cot.

Out of this distressing incident my old friend got one of his best stories. It lasted him a lifetime. He told it in all the best

---

31 The Spanish flu infected many of the troops in 1918, and Cy Corbett was hospitalized for it at least once, at Love Field and possibly again during his stint in Long Island.

public publishing circles of New York, to prove, I think, that there really does exist such a remarkable thing as one's Guardian Angel. And that sometimes they work in pairs.

But to get back to John Dewey and the camp newspaper, Colonel Dodd was as good as his word and gave my talented Virginia friend his orders within five weeks. I took over with an assistant, Larry Lehrbas, who was, later in life, to become a famous war correspondent. After one meeting with him, Dewey warned me, "Watch him! He's a Hearst type." I was too green to know what he meant.

Innate talent and early necessity had made Larry a "natural." He was very enterprising and very reckless; but he could smell a story a mile away. He outclassed me badly and made me look a little sick at my job. But he put life and nerve into the paper. And a deal of trouble, too, which he generally managed to sidestep. It mostly came down on my head, and did not enhance my image with the irascible Colonel.

Larry Lehrbas was the only Allied correspondent inside Warsaw when the Germans took it in the Second war. He had bylines all over the world. He was the slim, trim staff officer on McArthur's right as the general walked ashore on a Philippines beach in fulfillment of the General's vow to return. This pic also went around the world.

Larry looked me up in Chicago on his way home from the War. We had dinner together and a wonderful gabfest in a scrubby little restaurant in the Loop, for neither of us had much money. He was returning to his hometown, Great Bear, Utah—tired, sick and shortly to die.[32] Larry was not a great or even a

---

32   Lehrbas didn't die at that time, but in 1964, in Boise, Idaho. Lloyd Lehrbas (known as Larry) attended school in Wisconsin, and was a candidate for the Pulitzer Prize. He was famous enough to rate a long obituary in the *New York Times*. Several letters from Mr. Lehrbas were found in T.C. Corbett's correspondence file dated 1932.

good writer. But he had the newspaperman's one indisputable quality—being at the right place at the right time. He had had a life that was a reporter's dream come true.

I ran the paper as circumspectly as I knew how, until one unhappy day when Dodd, as commandant, was waited upon by a committee of five socially prominent Dallas women, wives of important businessmen, and whose lovely 17- and 18 year-old daughters had been violated, ravished, put in a family way by seven irresistible flying cadets from our field. They demanded blood. They screamed exposure and lawsuits. And to take the matter up with their senator in Washington.

Poor Dodd was in the spot of spots, and didn't know which way to turn. He was no diplomat, certainly. And not very resourceful. The army's attitude toward these things was no help either. It was, more or less, "boys will be boys." And let the local commander straighten it out. It would be a good test of his future promotability.

"The Engaging Five," Larry called them, and he seemed greatly amused. He tried out his considerable skill in working two or three accounts of the affair. They were colorful and somehow quite interesting, but they belonged far more in the *New Yorker* magazine than in the *Love Field Loops*.

I became convinced that the story needed some slight recognition in our paper. I played it down until it looked entirely innocuous. It was very brief. When I naively showed it to Dodd for his OK he looked over and I heard several old-time army curses which were entirely new to me. He finally sputtered

"For Christ's sake, Corbett, kill it! Don't print anything at all!" Then he looked at me oddly, as though remembering something.

"That's right! Your *overseas* orders are due!" He reached for a form and signed it. I left Love Field the next morning.

Incidentally, for the record, I never learned how Col. Dodd came out in the delicate affair of the Dallas daughters. But it couldn't have been good, for the next time I saw him, at Scott

Field in 1920, he had made it all the way down to technical sergeant.

Someone had hastily assigned me to the 346th Handley Paige squadron of the First Provisional Wing, London. Altho I had had most of the Pursuit training I was not cast down at being assigned as a lowly bomber pilot. In fact, I was jubilant at being at last on my way to see something of the main action before it was over.

The *Love Field Loops* was my first experience of the newspaper business, and it should have been my last. It should have told me how crazy the craft is, and how it was run by crazy people. It should have made me reconsider my sainted mother's words. She wanted me to be a pharmacist like our dour Scotch tenant, John McCluggage. She thought it a good, steady profession, and one that was not likely for a reckless boy to get hurt in.

A Visit to Sis Walsh

When my overseas orders came through, I wired Grace Walsh asking her if I could see her between trains. She said come: She met me at the railroad station in St. Louis about 9 p.m. She was not in a gay mood. Sis was at a boarding school, Concordia, and Grace had arranged for her to be at the main door where I could see her for minutes only. Mom waited in the car.

I was wearing my swanky new gabardine uniform made by the best tailor in Dallas. That, my silver wings and the shiny new black boots would surely impress my love, on my behalf. She came down promptly, greeted me in friendly fashion—but that was all. She was withdrawn and a little cold, as though her heart were not in the present scene. She wished me luck overseas, and added she knew I would have it. She told me not to get hurt, that she must go instantly, or get in trouble. She kissed me lightly on the cheek and was gone before I could say much or ask her to marry me. My first and last kiss from her. And thus ended my great love story that had really never begun. The whole thing was fast, and perfunctory. I felt that my life, unaccountably, had fallen on its face.

What had happened? This was not the lovely little girl I had met in old South Haven and was in love with ever since. This strange, oversize Amazon was not she, but where had she gone? This huge girl, very attractive, yes, but too overpowering for me, was certainly not my little water sprite with the devastating smile, the lovely body and the other-worldly charm that I once knew. Where was my Galatea, the subject of my many poems?

In September 1917 Sis had promised to knit me a sweater. On contemplating my upcoming departure into the army, I wrote the following poem, which appeared in the November 1917 issue of *Loyola University Magazine*.

To The Little Lady Who Knitted My Army Sweater

Thank you, fair lady, for the gift you send,
    The woolen-armored coat so warm and tight
    For me to wear against the winter's blight
When I am at the wars. Its charm will lend
Your Southland's sunshine where the blasts descend.
    When I stand sentry in the northern night,
    Alone beneath the watchful stars and bright,
I oft' will think me of a lovely friend.

Princess, your patient fingers linked a mail
    Of magic web, to be my guard until
        The guns are stilled and stemmed the crimson flood;
To bring me safely through the leaden hail
    And the red fields of death, if God so will.
        Or I will consecrate it with my blood.

—Cyril Corbett

ELEVEN

Fin de la Guerre
(The End of the War)

November 1918

One thing about being young, even a broken heart does not get you down for long. The train bore me to Chicago where I spent a day saying goodbye to my folks and then boarded its famed Century for New York. The only things I remember of that trip were two: first, in the smoking compartment I met a famous man and did not know who he was. He was William A. Brady, a famous theatrical producer. He was well known for large-scale theatrical productions and European imports. He had in mind, after the War, to put on a show of some kind with real airplanes. We chatted for an hour or two, and he wanted me to look him up after the war, which I never did.

The second thing—I was awakened in my berth about daylight by yelling outside the train. I raised the window curtain. The train was slowly crossing the main street of some town where hordes of people were shouting and waving their arms. It was 5:30 a.m. in Syracuse, N.Y. and it was our first inkling of the Armistice.

Two flyers in my car told me that the McAlpin Hotel was the place to stay, an informal town headquarters for our men, so I took a taxi there. I was shown to a room that was anything but fancy. When I came down, the lobby was crowded with youthful flyers and I was surprised to note that not all were second lieutenants. One young fellow came up to me, said he was from Montana and introduced himself as 2nd Lt. W.A. Jewett. He was lanky, intelligent and energetic. We went to dinner together, and then went out to see the Armistice Night celebration on Broadway, in Times Square.

The crowd was so dense you couldn't take a step in any direction. You couldn't see one square foot of vacant space. There was a deep overtone, a sea of human voices but you couldn't tell what anyone was saying. Suddenly my overseas cap was snatched from my head, and I couldn't see who grabbed it. Jewett, who was in a locked-in position near me, said it was a good-looking girl.

I can't remember how we extricated ourselves from the crowd. I don't think we did until after about an hour when it began to melt away. I found Jewett and he suggested that we go somewhere for the evening. He proposed the New Amsterdam Roof, an exclusive swank night club. How we got in on a night like that I have often wondered. Jewett seemed to have connections and we wound up at a table for two in the midst of a throng of theatre and society folk celebrating the return to life in a way only a little less raucous than on the street. He pointed out several famous people. There were several items of entertainment, including a Ziegfeld show. But nobody paid much attention. We had a couple of drinks and it cost us each $25, which I thot was a scandalous waste of money. Jewett was quite proud of himself as a bon vivant who knew his way among the sophisticated. At the end of the evening he said, "Corbett, I've got a very interesting proposition for both of us. Tell you tomorrow."

His proposition was startling. A warlord in China was hiring all the aviators he could get at $600 a month. Jewett said, now that the war was over we would shortly be discharged and free to go.

"What do you say, Corbett?"

"How do you know all this? Is it reliable?"

"I got it from my brother. He's with the government."

I said I didn't think my mother would like it. I'd have to think it over.

He said, "Well, don't be too long. When this news gets out a million shave-tails will be after the jobs."

I thought over the tempting proposition of $600 a month for just flying but didn't phone my mother. I knew exactly what her reaction would be. And the whole idea would greatly distress her. I admitted to myself that I was still tied to her apron strings. And it was lucky for me that I was. Poor Jewett went to China and I never heard from him. Somebody said he was killed in the first month.

A day or so later a half-dozen of us ventured out to Roosevelt Field for the first time, where we were assigned. The field was large and dismal, and it was a regular mudhole. There was a cot and quarters for us there, but no one stayed long if he were in funds. One good thing. It was in the sand there that I found my lucky goat shoe, which I still have.

I ran across some of the men I had known in Dallas for the simple reason that they were still there, waiting without hope for their overseas numbers to come up. The rumor among the men both at Roosevelt and the McAlpin was that we were *not* to be discharged immediately, but sent to Europe to fly patrol up and down the Rhine (actual story!). We waited and waited but nothing happened for ten weeks. Unexpectedly, on Feb. 4th we were given our choice of immediate discharge, or an equivalent commission in the Reserve. I chose the latter. And took the train for home, via Nashville, where I knew a pleasant young Southern belle who had a great admiration for flyers.

My impressions of the great city of New York were not good. The place was dirty, the people curt and why anybody would want to live there permanently was beyond me. There were too many people trying to live in too small an area. Consequently, everyone's nerves were ragged and their outlook pessimistic. Altho I had agreed to come back and see the Sunday editor of the *Times* about a job after the war, I didn't go or even phone him. I couldn't picture myself struggling in such an environment, even for the greatest opportunity in journalism. I hope he has forgiven me.

I can't remember where or how I met Eastman, a flyer like myself but a few years older. One of the many people who were always being kind to me. He was a native New Yorker and his civilian job had been as teller in one of the great N.Y. banks. I think it was the Chemical National. He had had an excellent salary and prospects of becoming a vice president. He was perhaps five or seven years older than I, but he was already spiritless and licked.

When I expressed some curiosity about how life goes on, day after day, in the great city, he undertook to show me. We rode the elevated railway to his apartment somewhere uptown. And I can still see the dismal picture of the grimy cars and dirty track while we waited on the platform. We had dinner at his house with his wife, also spiritless, and young child. They didn't seem to be having any fun, or have any hope in life. He told me he was making $10,000 a year (then a goodly sum) and paid $235 a month for the apartment. It was a cramped, two-bedroom affair, in a little less than good neighborhood. I wondered how lived all the people who didn't have a rich and influential uncle. Eastman was a nice fellow, and I lost track of him later, but I often wished I could do something for him.

I can't remember much else from that brief period in the great city except that there were always hordes of people wherever you went, and crowds of shave-tail young flyers around the McAlpin.

Once on the Long Island train (on the way to Roosevelt Field), I saw J. Fred Reeves, a flyer with captain's bars and a crushed English cap. Very swanky, indeed. He was talking a mile a minute with a group; besides, he didn't know me. He was another boy the Jesuits had high hopes for. A brilliant student, he had graduated ten years before and was practicing law with a top firm. But he wound up drinking himself to death, fifty years later, in an isolated farmhouse in Wisconsin. His life had been full of domestic strife— two women, one rich, divorces, uneasy reconciliations and no great accomplishments, no fulfillment of his youthful promise. The Jesuits have terrible luck! The devil always foxes them.

I was glad to shake the dust of New York from my feet, and return to the much saner and simple-minded Middle West.

* * *

Editor's Note: Upon being discharged from active service in 1919, Cy Corbett boarded the train to Chicago, but made a particular effort to travel through Nashville. There he visited Anna-Clair Glaser. Although we were unable to find a description of that actual visit, the piece below gives us an idea of his relationship with her.

~*1970 Recollection*

Southern Belle

Anna-Clair Glaser, a southern belle from Nashville, now long deceased, has been haunting me the last couple of days. I awoke this morning trying to recall a dream about her in which she seemed a trifle put out about something. But I couldn't determine what. And the incident bestirred me into writing this article.

Back in 1917 she was a classmate of Annis Cunningham, Vincent's sister, at a nun's school in Nashville, and was visiting in Chicago. She and Annis were bosom friends and visited each other's homes on vacation. It was apparent to me that she had

Vincent Cunningham's Mercer automobile. Included in the picture are Cy and Marie Corbett, Annis Cunningham, and two unidentified people.
(Courtesy of T.C. Corbett Family Archives)

a big crush on Vincent and his powerful, attractive Mercer car, as had my sister Marie, also.

    I thought Anna-Clair a charming girl. Very "southern"—very different from our northern girls, but I certainly was not in love with her. Sis Walsh, Dorothy Lyons and Louise Jefferson all had prior claims on my youthful affections. Besides, were not she and Marie battling in a quiet, feminine way for the hand of my classmate, who was a skilled engineer, had a way with cars and was undoubtedly quite a catch? I thot it all too complicated and tagged Anna-Clair as a good companion only.

    She was tall, slim and dark, nice looking, but not beautiful. She spoke well and with such a broad Southern accent as to sometimes not be quite understood. She had a wonderful sense of humor and an infectious laugh. She revealed a broader than usual outlook on life and I wondered where she had gotten it. All in all she was quite a charmer, but I recognized clearly that she was not my type in the matter of love and lifelong adoration. But an excellent companion she was.

Editor's Note: The following journal entry was Cy's initial description of Anna-Clair, written shortly after he first met her:

July 6, 1917

The girl from the South is a very agreeable and jolly sort. I like to hear her talk. Her version of the English language is very musical with its broad diphthongic vowels and immutable pronunciation. And lest of all it is entirely natural and spontaneous. The closest thing to it that I have ever heard was not French, but Greek, read by Mr. Bakewell, our professor last year, when he took me to his room one day and we discussed Demosthenes. The Southern dialect of English was even prettier, I think, than either the Attic or Doric dialects of Greek. I certainly enjoyed it. We all had a splendid time… I will hate to see Anna-Clair go south again, as she is a jolly girl.

~1970 Reflection:

We had many outings—picnics, short trips, sightseeing jaunts in Vincent's powerful Mercer. Hardly a half-week went by without a trip somewhere while we were waiting for the horrendous War to snatch us to an unknown fate. I can still see Mother's straightened face. Sometimes she went with us, but more often not. Generally the four of us—Vincent, Marie, Annis and myself—made up the party and its gay exchange of chit-chat.

On November 24th (1917) the War snatched me away, for good and all, from our gay foregatherings and as I learned, later from the pleasant Victorian way of life. The change of scene was profound. If I ever thot of those happy days again it was in short snatches while trying to keep my head above water in non-classical army courses.

I scarcely had time to think of my personal life and when I did it seemed like a dream in another lifetime.

When it seemed assured that we would pass all tests and get our wings and commissions, Bud Fisher (my army pal) and I went into Dallas one Saturday afternoon mainly to roam the business streets looking into shop windows as homesick soldiers are wont to do.

As told elsewhere in these remembrances, Bud stopped abruptly at a jeweler's window where he had spotted some small silver wings, one-half size replicas of the pilot's insignia. They were $5 apiece. Bud bought one for his girl back home. Thinking of my past social obligations, I didn't see how I could do with less than five. I bought three, which was all I could afford. Upon hearing my plight, Bud bought two more, saying I could reimburse him after payday.

The wings, how distributed—

Sis Walsh, the lovely beach nymph with whom I was still in love.

Dorothy Lyons, Louise Jefferson, and Anna-Clair Glaser (who were all trying their best to make me forget the above), and Marie, my sister, who would have never forgiven me had I left her out.

I had the gifts suitably wrapped and mailed to each girl. I wrote an accompanying note which read something like this: "I saw this trinket in a Dallas jeweler's window, and thought it an interesting memento of the stirring times we live in. Yours, TCC." On the note to Sis I added a line—"Sometime think of me, O heartless one." The acknowledgments I don't remember except that there was none from Sis.

Now, in the magic way that literature has, we have been carried more than 40 years into the future. World War I and its agonies and dislocations are a thing of the past and almost forgotten. Our world had changed unrecognizably. My Mother, Vincent and Marie are dead. I have married none of the girls of 1918, but Dorothy, whom I met at the *Tribune*, years later. At this moment we are driving to Florida for a short vacation. Going thru Nashville, something reminds me of Anna-Clair. Her old address popped into my newspaperman's mind—2102 Hillsboro Road.

We tracked her down without much trouble, considering the years that had flowed by. She was living by herself in a neat little house, near her brother (whom I have still to meet). She was a semi-invalid using a complicated crutch to get around on. A huge, mammy-type Negress came in for a couple of hours daily and cared for her. She had inherited some money from a wealthy aunt in California. And between that, her brother and her savings she managed to live quite comfortably. But she was very lonely.

We stayed over a day at the hotel in order to spend a couple of evenings with her. It reminded me of thirty years before. She was still a connoisseur of the droll. She could still look at life and its misadventures with high amusement and music in her laughter even when they applied to herself. She regaled herself with a complete account of her inexplicable bad luck with suitors down the years. Starting with Vincent, whom she really liked, she mentioned several local boys winding up with a wealthy, middle-age Nashville real estate operator, all of whom seemed to cool off mysteriously just before committing themselves to marriage. She concluded that there must have been something very wrong with her own attitude toward men and the Grand Passion.

I could have told her what it was but didn't, awaiting in some curiosity her own estimate of the situation.

Before we left, she said, "I want to show you something."

From a drawer, she produced my pair of silver wings, the ones I had given her so many, many years before.

PART THREE:

Returning from the War

TWELVE

You Can't Go Home Again

NOT MORE THAN A WEEK AFTER my discharge I arrived home to a round of parties at our home, and to a severe shock at my mother's health. She was pale and drawn and without much pep. The doctors made light of it, but she was not at all herself. I upended myself for giving her all the awful anxiety she must have had over me. The following is a contemporaneous diary entry explaining my situation:

Easter Sunday, April 20, 1919
Preface by the Deceased

The last words that I wrote in this diary were contained in the entry describing my last night at home—Nov 23, 1917—the night before my departure for the army. That was not quite a year and a half ago, and so much has happened since then, that it seems more than ten years ago. I believe that I have grown ten years older during that time, and that I have changed a great deal.

It was not altogether in a facetious mood that I wrote the title of this paper—for the old Cyril Corbett is dead forever. I don't know who I am except the person I have evolved into. I have completely reversed nearly every ideal I had before the war. My likes and dislikes have suffered a reversal too.

Probably foremost in the reader's mind is what happened to my blue-eyed goddess. I wish I had kept an account of the succession of events, as I am a little confused about when each happened. Sometime in my travel it was night; the silvery moon shown upon the beautiful grounds of Principia. Winding roads and early spring. Everything spoke of life returning. But our chevalier had death in his heart. He was going to the wars, and was as fully convinced that he was saying goodbye forever to the object of his grand passion, as he was of his very existence.

But I have looked thru the last volume of this diary and I find that already described. So that must have been during my visit there. This is the first time that I have tried to write anything except letters since that memorable night of November 23rd. So, my hand is out and this memoir of myself will be a hit-and-miss proposition.

What I started to say was that the old Cyril is dead. I attribute it chiefly to this: I was a hopeless idealist. I am not an idealist at all now. I love the spectre of Pierrette that I had built out of my own fancy. It was hopelessly unattainable. The war has done me a great service. It has disillusioned me. I have suffered greatly—never more than on that last night at home—but I count the price small. *I am not in love with Lillian Walsh, and never was.*

I was in love with a fictional character of my own imagination. That is one thing that makes me think that I may write someday. I am not in love with Dorothy Lyons—my ideals have changed and I find her very irritating sometimes. I am not in love with anyone.

How do you exist without a gleam to follow, you ask. My object in life now is first to make my Mother as happy as I can; secondly, to make the best of what I have—home, friends, books, brother and sister and comparative independence. I have learned how good food, drink, and sleep are, and how sweet life is; partly, I suppose, because I have often been deprived of the first three and came nearly being deprived of the fourth. I am happy enough to live and be with my own.

I have seen lots of girls with whom I could fall in love, but something has always checked me. I feel old, war-worn and world-wise. My enthusiasm has gone and I am contented to follow the golden mean.

One thing: I will never again feel that I really want to die. One day last August while I was flying near Love Field, my engine started to backfire badly. At the high temperatures of the weather then, it was suicide to let it continue. I lost no time in shutting off the engine and in getting down. But while I was still reaching for the throttle handle I thot, "In one old diary you wanted to die; you were disgusted and tired of life. All you have to do now is to hesitate a few seconds and you will die gloriously like a hero, falling like Icarus, and at the same time end the so-called miserable tragedy of life."

Then I saw the red glow of a library lamp (which has superseded the hearth fire as a symbol of love) and beside it was Louise, dark-eyed and fair of face, coming to greet me as I returned home from work years hence as a civilian. And very quickly I decided once and forever that I do not want to die. Life is good, if it is uncertain. I will play the game like I had to play it in the army (or die) and take what comes, like a good sport.

Reminiscences of the army are fast fading from me. I was discharged Feb. 4th, got home Feb. 26th, started to work March 31st. I have been working since, which amounts to three weeks. Physically, work is much easier than the army. When I come home at night, I am scarcely tired enough to sleep.

I am private secretary for Mr. Steger of the Steger Piano Co. My duties are not very important. It is not the job I would like to have but it will do for a start. Before the war, Charlie Byrne had promised me a favor when I allowed them to use a poem of mine in the company's advertising.

I remember one dreary day at the flying field at Mineola, Long Island, when the War was over and we were longing to be discharged, I found two telegrams in my mailbox. One from my Mother said, "Lamb Hayes is trying to get in touch with you."

The other from Lamb said, "Charlie Byrne says, 'Hurry home. We have a job for you!'"

I had completely forgotten the telephone call I received from Lamb Hayes prior to my being called up for Ground School. He had requested to use my poem "Music at Eve."

I replied to mother by wire, "Tell Charlie thanks, but I no longer write much poetry."

"They want you for confidential secretary to C.G. Steger, the piano magnate. This is your big chance!" C.G. Steger was getting impatient, Mother said. She thought I'd better do as they asked because at the moment there were 4,000,000 G.I.s being discharged and looking for work.

I told them to hold it for me. I would report to the piano works as soon as I got clear of the Air Service.

The poem that started it all:

Music At Eve

Music at eve. It soothes the troubled soul
Like sweet palm-odors that from censers rise.
Gently it greets the ears,—the very eyes—
Racked with the din of day, and makes them whole.

How silvery sweet these stringed accents roll
Soft to my touch, and up in glad surprise
To be again awaked, these human cries
Of pensive beauty or of thoughtful dole.

Wagner and Mozart, Mendelssohn and Liszt,
Verdi, ye are the poets of our race!
To ye the Muse must bow, your lips she kissed,

> And ye have seen all nature's radiant face.
> Vesper or Serenade in Venice mist,—
> Scents of the spring! What miracles of grace!
>
> —Cyril Corbett, U.S. Aviation Service (1918)

I'm getting $25 per week for my services. The money goes farther towards buying things than my $176 per month did in the army. Mr. Steger is a brainy man—both Stegers are. The rest are clerks—no brains, "more guts than a brass monkey." The people I am associated with are not interesting nor elevating. They are not like the men in the army. They were at least intelligent—and brave as the world. Byrne, though he got me in there, is egotistical, full of talk, selfish, overriding, and generally a low-brow type of Irish despite his college education. Sherwin Murphy & Ed Duffy are of course O.K.

The Steger Piano company occupies their own 17-story building on the edge of the Loop. Offices of the company occupy four or five stories. On my first day Lamb Hayes met me, and took me to meet Charlie Byrne, who first of all thanked me again for the poem. He then said he had gotten me this wonderful job, a magnificent opportunity for a bright young fellow like me because he believed in me. That nobody could tell where it would lead!

I had no shorthand and explained some doubts about my qualifications, which he waved aside with the remark that the only real requirement was brains, which I had amply demonstrated that I had. He took me up to C.G.'s office. He was a very dignified, very portly, wealthy Americanized German. He welcomed me home and to the job, and complimented me on my war record. (I didn't know I had one.) I was to start working with him tomorrow. My office was a little enclosure outside his office. I was to keep his personal records, answer some

> **Steger & Sons**
> PIANO MANUFACTURING COMPANY
> MANUFACTURERS OF
> THE CELEBRATED
> STEGER & SONS
> **GRAND AND UPRIGHT PIANOS**
> THE STEGER
> NATURAL PLAYER PIANO
> STEGER-MELOSTRELLE ELECTRIC PLAYER PIANO
> THE STEGER TALKING MACHINE
>
> OWNING AND OPERATING THE FOLLOWING
> SUBSIDIARY COMPANIES AND SELLING THEIR
> PIANOS AND PLAYER PIANOS:
> REED & SONS PIANO MFG. CO.
> SINGER PIANO MFG. CO.
> THOMPSON PIANO MFG. CO.

correspondence, occasionally take dictation, and come up with new ideas to benefit the company.

What I knew about being a secretary was a big minus. I struggled with all the details as best I could, and gradually learned to hate the job. C.G. himself, though, very tolerant to me, seemed to increase my general irritation with life. He came to work and departed at 4 p.m. in a big car with a liveried chauffeur, and belonged to several of the best clubs. I never heard him raise his voice but he created an atmosphere of fear. Around him his employees quaked and treated him like an Oriental potentate. It got my Irish hackles up, but I can see now that he put up with a great deal from me. One day he called me into his office and talked for almost an hour on what an employee must do to be a good employee and a success in business. I did not take a note but went back to my cubbyhole and put down his sermon in direct quotes almost word for word, Germanic expressions, slip ups, malapropisms and all. It was seven pages of single-spaced irony.

He must have guessed what I was doing, for he rang the buzzer and asked to see it. He got slightly red in the face but when finished he said, "Corbett, you have a wonderfully retentive memory. And being a reporter is your forte. I can see you are not cut out for a secretary."

He handed me the sheaf with a gesture of dismissal. Shortly thereafter he got a middle-aged, very efficient woman secretary from New York. She was the sister of the publisher of a successful trade journal whom he or Charlie knew. I was demoted to salesman, one of five, in the Display Department, the company's retail salesroom on the ground floor. It was a severe loss of prestige for me, but I thought I would give it a try just to see what comes. I averaged close to $500 a month in commissions.

I struggled to live thru those days, very unhappy although I was making about as much money as the Chinese warlord[33] would have paid for far more dangerous aviator work. The other five salesmen were all twice my age or more. A couple were alcoholics and the rest perfunctory and unimaginative, and licked by life's disasters. We took turns greeting the customers as they came in, sent by "bird-dogs" who scoured the foreign neighborhoods. They were Polish, Lithuanian, German and other nationalities who pathetically thot that a piano gave them a hint of home, gentility, and culture. Some could barely speak English.

We showed them the Steger second line—the Reed, the Churchill, or the Haverhill piano, made in the Steger factory but lower in price and quality than the main line. The other salesmen, somewhat impatiently, merely "showed" them the piano and, at best, struck a chord or two. When I demonstrated a piano, I ran through the first two lines of the "Rustle of

---

33 The warlord mentioned was Sun Yat-sen, leader of the Chinese Nationalist Party. He apparently wanted to develop his own air force to fight the communists.

Spring" or something from Trovatore. I played these things well and with feeling and ninety percent of the time it made a sale. My record quickly surpassed the other men until Charlie Crippen, a peppery little old-time piano man complained personally to C.G. that I was hogging the business. C.G. told him to become as good a salesman as I was, and then come back and state his grievance!

In spite of all this I was very unhappy and dissatisfied with my life. In those days when I was trying to become a civilian again, I had a recurring reverie. I was back in Texas in the frosty air of early morning, on the line, awaiting my turn to fly. The cacophony of motors idling or revving up was everywhere. Light was breaking across the Texas sky, leather-jacketed figures were all around, on hasty errands, and my old pal Bud Fisher was there, too, grinning at the scene and making some wisecrack that did not compliment the brass. That was life, I thought, at its fullest. Why did the scene have to change?

I would give anything, I thought, to be in it again, to be a lowly slave to it, waiting my turn to break my neck!

I thought, too, of joining the Jesuits. Had not tough old Father Lyons, the printer and Greek scholar, said to me, one time I was back on a visit, "Come back to us, Squirt. If you live. This is where you belong!" I told him I very probably would. But I knew I never would while Sis was in the offing. Much as I loved them, she always outweighed the Jesuits two to one.

In the retail sales department I averaged close to $500 a month, much to my and everybody's surprise. The Steger Piano company, when I came there, held quite a coterie of Loyola men. Besides Charlie, Sherwin Murphy was assistant advertising manager, Ed Duffy was assistant sales manager. Lamb Hayes had worked there before the war. I had known Charlie Byrne only as a great name. He was '06 and I was '18. I was restless and unhappy, and during this time my mother died. I welcomed a change of venue when the opportunity came, and went to Lyon & Healy.

Ed Duffy and Sherwin Murphy stuck it out until the Steger Co. fell apart in the Depression. Charlie opened a law office and was shortly appointed to the Illinois Commerce Commission.

Leo McGivena is back in the *Tribune* advertising department—He was in the army about seven months and got seven hours of flying. He very likely got cold feet and quit before he broke his neck.

Earl King is back, after experiencing 17 days of tank fighting. Ed Colnon is back and at Florissant. He stayed home ten days between trips. He was up here a good deal before he left and told me that he was disgusted with the marks of the beast in man—and didn't think he could be happy in the world, so he determined to give Florissant a try. He is a thoroughbred from the core. I should like to have known him better thru college.

June 7, 1919, Saturday

The further I go on in life the more I realize that we can never be sure of our conclusions. How intense, how earnest, how impatient we are in youth. I write these words today as a man knowing that there's nothing in life unattainable if our desires be but great enough. I know now that the system of Jesuit education is among the best; and, lastly, that my great ambition to write was not wholly infractious.

But with the coming of these comforting thots, I realize also that my idealism has departed. I was a hopeless idealist; I am now a practical realist.

The army did it. Before my eyes daily was a demonstration that idealism was impossible. My toes were treaded on sorely, at first. But through the instinct of preservation, I soon learned the trick of adaptability. The army did more to open my eyes, to give me a practical worldly education than all of my former life. I would have ruined my life; now I am in a fair way to make my way in the world.

I am not the same Cyril Corbett who wrote the *Journal of My College Days*. I have changed in every respect.

Hamlet said, "The Rest is Silence."

The Silence of Eternity is too soon upon us all. So, I am going to speak while I can. Let him who will, listen.

June 9, 1919

Yesterday, Sunday, I ran into Ralph Murphy, my Bunkie at ground school, and he reminded me that I owed him a dinner. I bet, he said, that a lot of us would be killed. He bet that we would all be back home again inside of two years. I had forgotten all about it.

Hard day at Stegers. This labor unrest is beginning to infect me, I am afraid. Marie and I went to a show this evening. Mother returned from the hospital Saturday and is feeling fairly well.

Yesterday met Curtis at the Jackson Park shelter. I can still see him getting ready to turn in. He had a bunk across the aisle from me.

Louise Jefferson, a Potential Suitor

Louise was very French-ish. Tall for a girl, dark hair and snapping dark eyes, she talked rapidly and seemed almost foreign. But she wasn't. She was a collateral descendant of the great Thomas Jefferson.

She had a mother, also French-ish, and a brother. They lived quietly in an expensive apartment on exclusive Hyde Park Boulevard. Louise was just through Normal (a teacher's college) and starting to teach school. I think it was Sherwin who introduced her to our crowd just before the War.

Louise had a quick mind and a vivid personality. She was not good-looking in the ordinary sense, or even very feminine. But her distinctive French air made her very attractive. On multiple dates she and I took to each other right away. I was fascinated by her talk of Montessori and the new educational psychologists. The girl was a "brain" without making a big thing of it.

She could go on, a mile a minute, on almost any topic. I had never known a girl like her. For one so young she knew a lot. She knew several French expletives, like "*Couchon!*" ("Rats!") which sounded like swearing, and she used them freely. She was vivacious and avid for life. And there was enough French in the Corbetts, a long way back, to establish a basic rapport of some kind between us.

I met her when things were in a mess. We went out a few times. I called at her apartment and met her mother, very intelligent, very French, very comfortably off from appearances. The father, now deceased, had owned a printing business.

"Ou-la-la, Monsieur! I think life is wonderful! Don't you?"

It was late evening. We were on 63rd Street, having just come out of a grubby little restaurant where we had cold grapefruit and coffee as an after-movie snack. She was bubbling over with life.

"Oh, I guess it is."

"Come, come, Corbett. You know it is! Wonderful, wonderful! You know something? I think men are wonderful, too!"

"That's kind of doubtful!"

"Listen, Monsieur Corbeau, *mon ami*. If it weren't a mortal sin, I'd love to be with the first man who'd let me. And it could be you, my friend! How would you like that, *chéri*?"

"Who wouldn't?"

"Well don't get your hopes up. We are not in Paree! And I don't want to go to hell! But what fun it must be to be a wicked woman without religion, in Paree! But for me only with you, my love!"

"Calm down, Louise. What you're saying is very probably a mortal sin."

She made French eyes at me, and a Gallic grimace. With a sharp toss of the head she indicated the spell was over.

Louise talked a lot about the Vieux Carré, the French section of New Orleans where her grandmother, Madam Gagne, who had lived in Paris, now lived; and where she had gone for lengthy visits. She rattled on about the great French restaurants there, Antoine's and Voison's. She speculated on how lovely life must be in Paris, both now and in the past of Balzac and Montaigne, while I wondered how it would be to live with this vivacious girl for a lifetime.

She told me Sherwin was a "stick," meaning dull and colorless, and was never really a beau of hers. It was only that her mother thought he came from a very good family and had asked her to be nice to him. She did have a serious suitor, however, a Chet Herrod, a nobody, really, who worked in a bank. He was too typically a businessman, staid, a little dull and generally unexciting. She confided to me that she much preferred a nice boy who had ideas, and an interest in people. And an imagination. And who was a little on the daring side. Someone (and here she blushed) like me!

There was a lapse in the story here—about two years. Until I was home again from the War, injured from my crash, cynical, and grieving over my Mother's approaching death. I had gone to work for the piano company, and found life hopelessly dull.

Louise called me at home one evening. I had not seen her since returning. She said she must see me, could I drop around? In my own troubles I had unintentionally been rude to her, so I invited her to the snooty and expensive Midway Gardens, an open-air night club much in vogue.

Over a small repast there, and half watching the floor show and interrupted occasionally by the aerobatic waiter, the famous Frank Le Buse, she told me that her erstwhile suitor, Chet Herrod, was home from the wars, and pressing her to marry him. What did I think she ought to do?

Herrod had a great war record. He had gone into the 149th

Field Artillery a private and come out a captain, after a number of bloody engagements, after being decorated on the field. I must confess that I was a little ashamed of my own record, having gotten no farther than Mineola, Long Island. It was perhaps the bleakest period of my life.

I told Louise that I would be frank with her. That my luck had run out. I was sick and hurt, and hopeless about life. That my business prospects were nil. That I was only waiting for my Mother to die. Then I intended to go to the Jesuits at Florissant, if they would take me. I told her that love was a crazy thing, but that if she wanted that kind of life, sexual, but decent, she should accept Chet, who was still lucky; after all he had done a great deal for his country, and deserved a break.

I can still see her dark, distinctive beauty. On first acquaintance it did not seem to be beauty, but distinction, individuality, and very Gallic. But it grew on you and soon you called it beauty for want of a better word.

She blinked and swallowed a few times, and said nothing that I can remember except after a moment, that it was time to go home. She married Chet and I never saw her alive again. She lived in a nice house that Chet was able to buy in Morgan Park, a far suburb, had three boys and died in child birth at 27.

Our courtship, if you can call it that, was brief and in a period of great upset and stress. It was probably a war casualty. She was such a vivid sincere person, I was never able to forget her.

I think that women should be given greater say in the matter of mate-choosing. They know, or sense, a lot more about life than men who are, after all, pretty stupid. And stupidity is always fatal to happiness.

THIRTEEN

The Death Vigil

From the Daily Journals of T.C. Corbett

October 8, 1973

My Mother

My Mother died 54 years ago today, in 1919. She was 54 years old! (Born in 1865.) I had sat up with her all night, this night. She moaned a little, not conscious. Around daylight I gave her her medicine. I put my arm around her shoulder to raise her a little for a more comfortable position. She died in my arms.

She was a dear woman, not very positive but capable of taking a firm stand now and then. At times she seemed overwhelmed by the energy of her children. She got along well with Aunty although the two were very different. They both had a large dose of common sense.

They had been very good-looking in their youth, I heard remarked more than once. They had one beau who came to pay a courtly call at least once a year, until the end of their lives.

Mother was a mild person; Aunty was a spitfire. But they saw eye to eye on most things. And both had a sense of humor.

They were not learned, or history-conscious, or psychologists. But they were excellent judges of the here and now. And of people they knew. They subconsciously rated them on their common sense, adjustment to life, and ability to cope. They were regarded as very smart and intelligent. And they had no personal idiosyncrasies. They believed in heaven and hell, God and the devil. And ordered their lives accordingly. Their first allegiance was to each other, and to us children and the home. They often feared how we would fare when they were no longer here to guide us.

They recognized that the world was a fast-changing one, but they felt fairly secure in the pleasant enclave they had built at 6318-20 Greenwood Avenue, Chicago, Illinois, in the short years from 1907 to 1919.

The days, weeks, months and years tumble by in their haste. And nothing very recent seems as solid and real as those days of my youth spent under the mantle of their gentle love and care.

I pulled out my old diary, which was packed away in my steamer trunk. I found the following account, as if I had been led to it by some unknown force:

My beloved Mother was in Mercy Hospital. Old Dr. Morgan, a family friend of my parents' youth, called me aside one day and told me she was not going to get well. She had cancer. It was an awful blow, for I couldn't imagine life without her. She was sent home from the hospital to be in bed all the time, where she faded away a little each day in quiet suffering. Everything was going wrong. Life was becoming a disaster.

September 14, 1919

Dejected again. My life seems a complete failure. I have striven greatly—for nothing. Mother is very bad. Everything I love is slipping from me. In these days I often think that it was my fate to die in the war, and through some adverse chance I did not. It certainly would have been better.

Picture: a young man of high ideals struggling through college—Merlin and the Gleam—the great desire just short of attainment. War—Aviation—Death. Here would be a photograph of a promising youth cut short. There is something tragically beautiful in unfilled desire and ideals, unfilled after great striving, through no fault of the striver—the old Greek idea of an adverse Fate and tragedy.

Now they are as ever unfilled—I who wrote on July 6th:

"Dreams and visions are being filled for me beyond my wildest expectations" but have tasted the wormwood.

Mother—my work—abandonment of my striving after a career—friends—everything gone. Each day is a dreary drudgery.

September 16, 1919

Father Broderick anointed Mother this afternoon. When I came in, she didn't tell me. Aunty did later. When I said, "Father Broderick was here this afternoon," she said, "Oh what did she tell you that for? It will spoil your supper."

I asked if it frightened her.

"No," she said, "but don't let it frighten you, honey."

In former years I often thought, "What if Mother should die?" I thought I would die too. Life is impossible without her. She is a living saint for sanctity and a soldier heart for fortitude. My heart is aching with an actual physical ache. Oh God, God, God, is all I can think to say.

September 18, 1919, Thursday

Today I made my first sale, second sale and rented a piano all before noon.

September 21, 1919, Sunday

All salesmen and Mr. Byrne congratulated me on my first sale.

While very sick, and in bed today Mother heard an airplane. She said in horror: "Oh, that horrid plane."

September 26, 1919, Friday

Last night Mother said when Bebe Stanton brought her flowers:

"Oh, if I could bloom again, like the flowers."

Tonight she said to me:

"Cyril, I'm afraid my long fight is over."

Marie said that Mother talks in her sleep. The other night she said aloud:

"Was he a first or a second?"

Marie woke up and asked what she said.

"Was he a first or second lieutenant?"

"Who?" Marie asked.

"Becker."

Becker is a boy who bunked next to me at the University of Illinois Ground School. He called here a day or two ago. I was out and Marie talked to him and told Mother later that he called.

Mother is very weak. She had wonderful vitality and has fought heroically.

"Only God and I know what I have suffered," Mother said to me tonight. "This is what I have dreaded all along—getting so helpless."

This morning I slept after the alarm had rung and she rang the little bell I bought her. I jumped out and ran in. She asked me if I hadn't overslept. In the greatest pain and weakness she always thinks of others.

Tonight I found out that Mother and Aunty went to

Communion for me almost every day while I was at war. I was not worth it.

September 27, 1919, Saturday
Mother is very bad. She sleeps nearly all the time. She had been taking a great deal of strychnine. When I told her this evening that I had sold a player piano she smiled sweetly and said, "God bless your heart."

She is very thin and emaciated. She hasn't eaten anything for two days. The wrinkles are deep in her face and her cheekbones stand out. Her hands move in her sleep, in little gestures of despair. It is nervousness or the medicine. She is dearer to me now than ever.

September 30, 1919, Tuesday
Mother very bad yesterday. I stayed home from work and Marie stayed in bed as she is nearly sick too. Toward evening I went over to the University of Illinois Medical School. Loyola M.S., Rush M.S., University of Illinois College of Pharmacy. Went chiefly because I am very restless. Impossible to enter with college physics lacking.

Today: Mother much better. Tonight I carried her from the parlor to her bedroom.

Rented a piano today. Adams left. Lowenthal, a dealer, congratulated me warmly on my first sale and gave me some valued advice. They are all very kind to me. I often think that there is nothing that means anything to me without Mother. I will not care for success. A barn to sleep in and a crust to eat. But something—the hopelessness of it all—drives me on.

October 4, 1919, Saturday
On Wednesday about 3 p.m. they called me home from work. When I got there, Mother was sitting in the parlor literally gasping for breath. Marie, Bus and Aunty were crying, the Brannans were there, Carrie Stanley and Dr. Herriman. Father

Erban was going through some kindness of Providence so I called him. He came in and prayed for Mother and let her kiss the indulgenced cross. I got my crucifix, the one Father Mathery gave me at Florissant when I was in the army and held it in readiness. Her face was death and when she stopped gasping I watched a little vein in her neck for the last heartbeat. They got faint and I promised God that if He would give her twenty years of life I would be a priest.

Thursday, Friday and Saturday I did not go to work. Thursday Mother's condition was slightly improved.

Friday, Father Broderick came and gave her Holy Communion. She had much difficulty in swallowing. When he left, she kept repeating, "I don't see why I should go and leave my honeys." Later, when I was fixing her covers, she said, "Oh, Tom, dear." (Thinking I was my father.) For me that is the finest compliment I can ever receive.

This morning she asked several times if we were not "in a strange country." Her words are often unintelligible and she leaves off sentences in the middle and later can not remember what she was saying. She wakes up and says, "Oh, I guess I am talking."

Father Hishen came and prayed over her and told her that she had never done anything but serve her creator and her family. He called her dear. He told her to compose her mind and not to let any little thing worry her.

When he had gone, she seemed bewildered and asked, "What does it all mean? The priest... and the doctors... I can't go and leave my darlings." Later she called us in and after settling the business of her estate told Bus that he had always been her comfort, and Marie, that she had taken care of her (Mother) long and faithfully, and me, that I must learn to control my temper. "If you ever speak a cross word to the children, remember that I hear you." Tonight she said when Marie and I were in the room with her, "What would I do without my honeys?"

Sometimes she speaks confidingly in whispers about the

wanderings of her fevered imagination and it is with the voice of infinite patience and suffering.

October 13, 1919, Monday
"Could You Not Watch One Hour With Me?"
Mother died Wednesday, October 8, 1919, at ten minutes to 1:00 p.m. She was buried Saturday, October 11, at about noon. My last evening with her was October 4, Saturday. I could not write. Words died in my throat as I saw her die. She was unconscious Tuesday and Wednesday. What happened Sunday and Monday I forgot except that Monday morning I went to the store for a short while. Before I went, she bade me goodbye. Her heart looked into mine through those tender eyes and that was really the last time she was fully conscious. I could not bear to say goodbye and I choked on the words and kissed her several times returning. When I got back she seemed surprised, and I told her they had sent me home till she was better. I stayed up with her Monday night till 12 or 1 and then Marie sat with her from 1 till 6. Mother vomited a great deal—a reddish dark fluid which was blood.

Tuesday she stayed in bed all day—the first day, I believe, that she did not sit up for a little while. Tuesday night she wandered a great deal and insisted that she wanted her coat, and that she must be going home. We told her that she couldn't put her coat on and she said, "You're foolish; I can't go this way in my nightgown." Her speech was low and in whispers and very often the sentences broke off before they were finished.

I wanted to humor her so we put her coat on. She wondered about the fur cuffs which she had removed sometime before. She thought they were on the floor till I reached down and pretended to pick them up. Then she wanted to get up. She kept on repeating, "I must be going, I must be going," in that heartbreaking whisper. I helped her walk to the door and back though she didn't want to come back. She wouldn't take off her coat till she got to sleep.

We gave her strychnine tablets at 10:30. She vomited them and later we gave her more. Aunty was going to sleep till 12 and Marie till 3. When they got up, I told them to go back to bed. Something inspired me to watch that night though I was dead from fatigue. I gave her the tablets at 2:30 and at 5:00. First, I gave her a drink of water and then talked and pleaded with her to take the medicine and finally told her that the doctor would have to come and give her a hypodermic. She seemed to come to for a moment, look at me and then swallowed the medicine. At 2:30 she vomited it almost immediately but not at 5:00. I sighed with relief when I had given her the medicine but did not realize that by it I made her last moments inarticulate. I will never be willful again or insist on anything no matter how much I "know" I am right. I sat beside her till I fell asleep several times during the night and then paced the hall saying my rosary. I left her once to go to the bathroom and once to drink a cup of coffee. Later on I took some of my old notebooks out of the bookcase and started to read essays I had written in college. I could not watch one hour with thee, my Mother, who had watched with me for 24 years.

She moaned continuously during sleep and kept throwing her arms out of the covers, which I suppose made me wretch, anxious to give her the medicine. At 5 she looked at me so reproachfully after pushing it away several times that I will never forget—those dear eyes dimmed by suffering.

At 7 in the morning I went to bed and slept till 12. I got up and started to take a bath. Buster told me I had better hurry in. I jumped out of the tub, put on my underwear and a bathrobe and ran in.

She was holding a crucifix. I took it from her hands and touched it to her lips and held her hand. Then she made a high-pitched cry and there was a gurgling sound in her throat. Her head fell to one side, her mouth was partly open and her dear eyes were mostly closed. We all cried. I petted her head and pleaded for her to live—my dear Mother. The doctor came in, looked at her and said it was all over. I kissed the dear dead lips, closed her eyes and crossed her hands on her breast, and remembered when I was a little boy she used to sing a little song or talk about who would cross her hands on her breast when she was dead.

That was my saddest and bitterest hour. I crouched on the floor where I was and as I was, at the head of her bed and cried from my soul. I thought of giving her the medicine against her will and that my heart would break. The doctor said it was better so as otherwise she might have died struggling.

Aunty, Marie and Bus had been in the room with her all morning. I had been alarmed on waking to find her still unconscious. We sent for the doctor then but he was not in. I cried there on the floor while the doctor tied the death bandage around her head, and it was the darkest hour. God, I would gladly have died for her or with her. Strong was the Mother's love for the first born. I loved her more than anything on this earth or even God, and the reason I didn't love her more was because I was incapable of greater love. My soul was seared when my heart was still tender and since I have been odd and queer but honestly I can say that I love her more than other man or woman, or happiness or life or God or anything.

And now she is dead and gone from me. The only reason I do not cry myself to death is because I can't. Something has snapped and I cannot think about her anymore.

The Funeral

A multitude of friends, even some we didn't remember, gathered at her funeral. Tough aging Fr. Hishen shed a surreptitious tear. My life was torn wide open at the loss of this brave and understanding woman, and it is quite right to say, it would never be the same again. The night of her burial I couldn't sleep. I swear I could feel the cold of the grave assailing my flesh.

A delegation from Stegers had come to the house: Charlie Byrne, Lamb Hayes, Sherwin Murphy, who was assistant

Lizzie Keenan Corbett (1865–1919)

advertising manager, Ed Duffy, assistant sales manager, both Ignatius boys, and two pretty girls, secretaries whose names I can't recall. Several of the Jesuits and boys I had known from school were there. Two or three old friends of my father's from the Holden Shoe Company days of 15 years before showed up, looking worn and on the edge of the grave themselves. Both old and new friends were sincerely devastated at the passing of this brave woman who, in some mysterious way, left courage to all who knew her and was a pillar of faith and staunchness. Thus died "Lizzie" Keenan, of the little understood disease that strikes down so many, cruelly and with great suffering. I asked myself where God was, and decided for many years to come that he did not exist at all. That we were all accidental creatures, the result of some chemical action on a freakish, accidental planet.

October 27, 1919, Monday

Bud Fisher came last Friday night and departed Sunday morning. Toots took us riding after we had called at Dorothy's. Saturday afternoon and evening Bud was sick and had Dr. Herriman.

I took Bud to the Union Station Sunday morning; bought his wife two boxes of California chocolates and he left.

So soon departed, and in me was a dull pang. This man with whom I endured Titanic labors and risks and who I have often longed and longed to see, could move me to only a dull pain of loss at his departure. I have lost the facility to feel.

October 30, 1919, Thursday

Oh, my dear, dear Mother, my heart aches tonight. I have never felt so desperate and abandoned. I thot of ending it tonight. The lake is not far. It would be relief to be rid of this agony of life. I have thot of that last night, when I watched with you. The knife turned in my heart and my grief and despair were more than I can tell.

God seems to have abandoned me. I am outcast and alone and even my faculties are scattered. I cannot think. I am not myself, sometimes I cannot even feel the pain of grief for numbness. Why I do not curse myself and die I do not know. I am at the end of my endurance. I realize now that I love you, Mother, more than anything in life. Why should I work or study or carry on or obey that stirring impulse now that you are gone? It's all for nothing. If you read this, guide me, Mother, please, from heaven. I am on the rocks.

FOURTEEN

Job Hopping the Way to the *Tribune*

WHAT COULD I DO? I did not know. One lunch hour I ran into Bob Wenban on the street. I had known him slightly somewhere in the Air Service. He lived in Lake Forest, the wealthiest suburb, which was all urbanely and well-built. We told each other how life was treating us. He was leaving a writing job at Lyon & Healy's, a department store of music, across the street, yet, from Steger's. He was going to Harvard, to attend "Baker's 47 class" in drama writing.

"How wonderful," I said. "Could I get your old job at the music store?"

He took me back. I met his boss, a Mr. Wessell, and got the writing job at $35 a week! It was a mailing piece in color, a blurb about the latest phonograph records, sent out once a month to a huge mailing list. An easy job that took only a fraction of my time. I started at Lyon & Healy on January 19, 1920, and liked the pleasant atmosphere of easygoing laissez faire with a touch of melody and artistic folderol.

But I soon heard of another writing job that paid more, $45 a week, with Hearst's *Herald Examiner*. I applied for and got the job. I now understand, I think, how Hearst could be the enterprising journalist he was and not make his string of papers pay (their employees) very much. He was clever and intelligent. He nursed several great names: Loretta Parsons, Walter Winchell, Damon Runyon, and many others to fame in a big way. He understood their genius, was tolerant and generous to them, giving steady encouragement of the right kind. Yet his shop, run at a distance thru small lieutenants, what I saw of it, was a mess.

Our function was to work with the retail shop salesmen, helping them sell, then writing ads that would "pull" business into the specialty shops that were, to begin with, sold on the *Tribune*. Hearst got but a fraction of the outstanding business and among his men it was a dog-eat-dog fight for sales and credit. They all knew that every eight months there was a general housecleaning, and that they would lose their jobs. It made for a nasty sort of competition combined with fear.

April 7, 1920

Five months have passed—almost to the day—since the last entry. I felt lonesome, melancholy and alone, so I pulled out this old book. I had regarded it as closed forever.

Many changes have come since the last writing. As I write, Buster (my younger brother) is playing on his saxophone. I am tired—tired to death. All I live for and think of is rest. It is heaven to me.

I am working for the *Herald Examiner* as a copywriter in the merchandising department. Left Steger Jan 19th. Then worked for Lyon and Healy till March 1st. There is one thing still the same: life seems barren and empty—altho I am making great efforts to improve it. The bottom seems to have dropped out. I can't get my feet on the ground. Am going to take two months' vacation this summer and get back my old point of view, the old cheerfulness and faith and the old courage. Courage, *mon enfant*, hold out a little longer and we shall gain the crest.

October 4, 1920

I have had two operations: for appendicitis, and one on my nose. Have to have two more: tonsils and adenoids. I will not work until I am better.

I have left the *Herald Examiner*, but I have made good, I think, as a copywriter. High-water marks last Sunday, when I had a half-page ad in both papers. I stayed with the job until the next eight-month housecleaning, when I was fired.

We have a Chandler (motorcar).

Marie is engaged to Vincent Cunningham.

I have suffered Hell in the last year. The agony of grief has abated somewhat. But I have been acting strangely lately; I fear that I am losing my mind. I fear I may be going insane. I wonder where I'll be in six months from now. Some possibilities:

1. Home, as now; 2. Florissant; 3. West; 4. Asylum; 5. Dead.

October 13, 1920, Wednesday

Returned at 5 this afternoon from a trip to Rantoul[34] and Champaign. What is wrong with me? Will I never lose this old heartache? As the years go on it mounts higher. A little more and life will be insufferable. It is almost so now.

At Rantoul last Saturday while in the air I looked down and almost wished to crash to put an end to this old agony. To bed, to sleep, and oblivion.

October 23, 1920, Saturday

I Am Diagnosed With Intense Mental Depression

Last Monday, I underwent another operation—tonsils and adenoids this time. Since May 27th this year, I have had four operations in five months: Appendix; Frontal Sinus; Tonsils; and Adenoids. I have worked thru all of them.

---

34 Rantoul, Illinois, was home to an Army Air base established in 1917. Cy was still in the Reserves and occasionally flew airplanes until 1936.

I feel very bad today—weak, pain in the back, nauseated. And worst of all, there seems no prospect of betterment in the future. Dr. Morgan says that there is nothing organically wrong with me—heart and lungs good. But I am suffering from *intense mental depression*. He said I ought to work outside all the time but it was imperative to do it for a year anyway.

~*1970 Recollection:*
The Journal of Commerce (Began work Nov. 1, 1920)
I was beginning to lose faith in myself. I knew I had lost my punch and personality and, I was afraid, hope. I stayed home two days doing nothing, when I got a phone call from Reed Fisher, Bud's older brother. He said he had just taken a job with a new newspaper, *The Journal of Commerce*, and he thought there was one there for me. Should he set up an interview?

I went down to the address in the Loop that Reed Fisher[35] gave me and saw a Mr. José Borhn, a grey-haired Cuban, who was the managing editor of the new paper. He was well spoken, scholarly, and I learned later that he had degrees from Harvard and Amhurst. Borhn had been managing editor of the *New York Journal of Commerce* before coming to Chicago to start the new publication. He asked me a few questions about my education and army experience and previous jobs. And I was hired, at $50 a week, to be a staff reporter. I went to work the next day.

I remember Aunty remarking, when I told her that evening, that I was terrifically lucky about jobs.

The working offices of the paper were in a third-floor loft (no elevator) in a wholesale section, on Austin Avenue, north of the Chicago River. The section was bare of any adornment and had a poverty-stricken look.

A gruff elderly man was the city editor, under whom I worked. There was only one private office, Borhn's, at the head of this large room full of desks and typewriters. Reed Fisher was

---

35   Brother of Bud Fisher, Cy's army friend.

a financial reporter and wrote all his stuff in longhand. Paul Martin, who I was to know later, was drama critic, wrote book reviews and sat in on the copy desk. Capt. McMillan, very British, and Capt. Russell, very Irish, were general reporters, rewrite and copy desk men. Most of the editorial men met at the Press Club at 5 p.m., had a meal and magnificent gabfest before reporting for work at 6:30 p.m. McMillan had been with Allenby[36] and had known Lawrence; Russell had been in France and in the Irish rebellion. The first lewd tales they told were vivid and unforgettable. Newspapering in their lives was a pretty tame *reductio ad absurdum*.

I really did not know much about reporting for a big-time metropolitan daily but the city editor A.B. Frost was very kind to me. And I managed a story a day, big or little, which kept up my end of the bargain. Then I was given an assignment to interview Maclay Hoyne, the state's attorney who was in some crucial legal spot and home with a cold. I rashly broke into his house and found him upstairs in his bedroom with his feet in a pan of water, drinking hot whiskey. After his surprise, he laughed heartily, said I was lucky he hadn't mistakenly shot me. And then he gave me the story. It made column one, on the front page and was a citywide beat. None of the other papers had it. I got a byline, my first, and a raise to $55 a week. After that, frequent bylines.

The Pain of Life

November 17, 1920

I am now realizing my career—what I have dreamed of and sacrificed so much for; and I would trade it for a nickel. What will fill this restless heart? I have burst one more illusion—that I want to work on a newspaper.

---

36 Field Marshal Viscount Allenby commanded T.E. Lawrence (Lawrence of Arabia) during the fight against the Ottoman Empire.

What will fill this restless heart? A career, love, fortune, adventure or death? I have been desperately unhappy and lonely. I have suffered a hell of remorse and bitterness. It seemed at times that I must take my life to be rid of the dreadful burden of life. And I lived from day to day. But no more of myself. This is a painful slice of life. There must be others who are happy or at least contented.

December 16, 1920, Thursday

An ancient melancholy, old as the earth is old, seems to have claimed me for its own. I work, never play, and after work when I have a few moments to think, the old hurt opens again. It is some immemorial grief that time cannot dull and I doubt if hell can surpass it.

It always returns with thought. While I work a stupor, a certain forgetting possesses me; I am almost a different person with other problems. But with thought and remembrance comes the old agony.

I most certainly have a serious quarrel with life. I am alone utterly, without friend or enemy. The past is full of painful memories; the future distrust. The present holds nothing but ten hours of work every day, and after that, physical exhaustion. I love nobody, I hate a great many persons and things, including life. I see no solution ahead except a dogged perseverance in what I am doing for five or ten years, the most abject kind of self-denial, and then when my youth is gone, I will at least be independent of the economic scheme.

If I follow this line, I am almost certain to come to a bad end. When I quit working I will probably quit living. My few friends will have left me, not understanding (and I do not blame them) and I will be more alone than now, if that is possible.

Why don't I kill myself? I would have long ago if I did not believe in hellfire. So long as I have already suffered so much, why continue it after death? My only chance of happiness seems to be then.

When I come home every night, I am in a state bordering on physical exhaustion. I eat a piece of cake and drink a glass of milk; that is all.

Many times, I find myself mummering involuntarily in the throes of some painful thought—O Christ.

FIFTEEN

Newspaper Life

MAYBE EIGHT OR TEN MEN sat around the big table at the Press Club, eating breakfast and telling stories. These sessions were fabulous. They were a close-up view of a glamorous world I had never seen, told mostly by the two ex-captains who vied with each other for the appreciation of their audience.

Paul Martin, twenty years older than I, let me review a few books and took me with him several times to his first night stints at the theatre. Life had become more tolerable, even a little interesting when I got a call from someone at the *Tribune*. McGivena, my school friend, whom I had given the wild motorcycle ride in Texas, worked on the *Tribune* in the paper's own publicity writing department. He had often urged me to try for a spot on the paper. And when Hearst fired me I had filed an application with them. I saw Broadfuehrer, head of the paper's Copy and Art Department, and was offered a job as advertising copywriter for $50 a week. I told him I was getting that now. His reply, "But not from a *great* newspaper." I told him I needed to think it over.

That night at work I told Frost and Borhn I had an offer from the *Tribune*, Borhn said, "Go out to dinner with me. Ten o'clock."

When we were seated, he said,

"Now you young damn fool, don't tell me you're like all the rest and are going to fall for their glamour bit."

I said, "But it's a chance to make big money, and I need it. The girl I want (*Sis Walsh*) takes a lot of money!"

He shook his head, sadly. "But I was going to send you to Washington to understudy Bill Ayers, our man there, who's only so-so. You are a much better writer. Won't you reconsider?"

"Mr. Borhn," I said, "I like working for you. Everyone there has been awfully kind. But I love this girl more. I will surely lose her without money."

"Have it your way, young fellow. But I hate to see a talent like yours go to waste. They will simply bury you. They will pay you fairly well, but you will never be a big name in journalism! I know exactly what they will do to you! Col. McCormick is the only notable on that paper. He sees to it. And God knows he is no writer. You haven't a chance there. When you have learned that a beautiful woman who requires money is not the most important thing in life, look me up. We will have dinner again—if I am still alive."

I said that I was grateful for his interest, but that I had to go.

My dear little grandson, can you imagine anyone as dumb as I was?

* * *

January 26, 1921
On the Occasion of Louise Jefferson's Wedding

Louise was married this evening to Chester Herod. Marie and I were present at the reception along with many others—flowers laughter lights life hope happiness—these things are very strange to me. I can't describe it.

Louise kissed me as I came in. The first and last time. She was very attractive. Chet was calm, quiet. There were three flats open and many, many, friends.

We came home. Buster and I exchanged some bitter words as we put the car away. My fault, possibly, in my heart I was cursing creation.

Aunt, Marie, Bus and I talked a while in the parlor. They did not care to go to the show with me. I went alone. Afterwards—home. Another fit of hatred.

Out and walked till 11 o'clock. Home. Writing now. This is the end of this diary notebook. So why not foot up the total? A Reckoning:

I am a failure—total and complete.

I am paying off an ancient curse.

I am going mad. The bitterness and hatred I cherish for myself, my own and the world are alarming—that is why I say I must be mad. Walking tonight, the emotion was so high I could have shrieked—but I sobbed.

What is the reason? Everything has gone wrong. I am a bundle of vain desires and hopes that have languished and died. As I look back over my 25 years, the whole of life seems one long pain and mental wretchedness.

I swear, the only thing that keeps me from making tonight the end of this miserable life is one last hope that my suffering may be repaid in heaven. Otherwise an army colt and one cartridge would end my present unhappiness. Family, friends, hope—nothing would deter me.

Where this wretchedness started, I do not know. It seems I have been hurt since I can remember. O Christ.

It is not because of Louise. I liked her but did not love her. Why? Because of the *ancient trauma*—the old hurt, the wound that would never heal. The obsession that was growing. It is my circumstance, my birth, me. There was something wrong from the beginning. I have all but cursed my father and mother for even bearing me. Today I would thank them for the doom of oblivion. I wonder if my father dreamed of such a miserable spawn.

In 1911 I met Sis Walsh in South Haven. She left and

someone turned a sword in the trauma. The cut grew uglier and more gangrenous each succeeding year. In spite of this handicap I persevered through college, and then the war.

In the excitement and action, the ever consciousness of the wound left. I was a whole man for a while and though rich in hardship and danger I was happy as never before in life.

Then the armistice, home, work, Mother's death, my four operations and all concomitant wretchedness, the lake, the loss of my job at the Herald. My present job. A quick succession of events trending downward. I am making almost twice as much money as a year ago but I hate life five times as much.

I have come home nights and wept alone and wretchedly, from my soul as only the damned must weep. I have drained the cup of bitterness. Can't believe that many men have suffered as I, because without the restraining motive they would die.

I write more calmly now. The razor edge of pain across the mind seems to diminish. But to resume, Louise and I had many talks about 1½ years ago. She said she must decide whom to marry as it was time and Chet wanted an answer. I liked Louise, maybe I loved her, though I think not. But could have. She said one time I would never love anyone because I wouldn't let myself. She was right.

I was conscious then of the great obsession that must be cleared up. If I married her, I knew that I would only make her unhappy. You see, it is the consciousness of the trauma, the mind wound that is always present. And so, it passed and she married Chet. She is a great girl and we might have gone far and accomplished much. But curse the day I acquired the trauma.

I can see myself never marrying. I will be unhappy thru life and accomplish nothing because I will be a wanderer. I am old now; my youth is all but fled and I have not enjoyed it. My face is beginning to show the marks of wear. I have put off the study of law each year thinking to have my fill of happiness while young, for I worked so hard before.

My sister and brother hate me. My brother will not sleep with me tonight. My sister's last words were those of abuse. Aunty is indifferent and doesn't care. Home life is wretched. Bitterness on all sides, slovenly housekeeping. My sister stays in bed most of the day and often when I come home the work is undone and there are dirty dishes around. My room is always untidy, unkempt and I do not have the courage to do it myself, which is one reason I can't find a little comfort in reading or writing. In other words, things have gone to hell. But more than that, I hate the smug satisfaction with the state of things and secondly their indifference to my mental suffering.

I hate mediocrity of any kind. I hated it in school. I was not mediocre. I led the class the first year and that seeming too bourgeoisie I devoted my time to the magazine but still remained among the scholastic leaders. I did not want to be mediocre in the army. I wasn't. I couldn't stand a mediocre job. I quit. I have now a job that is not mediocre. I quit Lyon & Healy, and the *Herald*. I am earning a living with my pen. It is something to be a rewrite man on a metropolitan newspaper at 25. I am making more money than many who were working before I started high school. And I still refuse to be mediocre. God may punish me for this pride, but it seems that I can't help it. It is against my nature.

My father was not mediocre. I can read it from his life, -long separated as it is from the present. He fought the good fight and failed to win ultimately not because mind or courage was lacking but because the greatness of the task overpowered him physically. And he went down fighting. He suffered. His doctor has told me of spells of desperate despondency—(and we are in that race today).

Out of the old mind-wound grew the promise I made to myself. I would search men's souls and plumb the depths of their despairs because I had been there myself. Like the last Spartan at Thermopylae every stroke would tell and time would pay dearly for the scar it had put on my soul when I was born. Men would remember me, and my name would not die.

Hollow satisfactions, but time would pay the last farthing. I planned, I wrote, I went to college, to work to earn independence and leisure to write. And all along it was a drive through misunderstanding, privation, unhappiness, doing without what a normal youth seeks, and loneliness.

I never failed in school, never once. I'll shout it to the stars. My intelligence and industry were of front rank. I never quailed in the army. My courage stood the severest tests. Unhappiness. Why? Because of the ancient trauma.

I have passed up normal pleasures—anything that would fasten ties on me to keep me from my work. I left the pursuit of money to follow practical letters (and found more money). Money, money, it buys everything wanted poignantly. It would erase the trauma—make me forget these damn, damn wretched years. It would give me leisure, environment, travel, acquaintance, everything.

Remove the trauma is the answer. How? That takes money, then work. When that fails you, choose again. Work, Work, dare and forget. That's the answer.

What will you do tomorrow? Start in the old treadmill again. I wish for a change.

God looks down on mortal anguish and probably marvels at the stupidity of it, the solution is so easy. If I could only know it and find courage to apply it!

Bitterness, tears, hatred, envy and despair, I have known you too well. I want to know love, hope, ambition, contentment, happiness. I want to be normal and satisfied and even mediocre, if that will help.

My family will not help me. That is certain. I am going to have outside friends, go visiting, have company, go away. I write so as never to forget they have been fiendish in their indifference and smugness. I will remember it. They are not worthy to be placed first—before myself as I have always done.

I will watch out for myself and not sacrifice my own pleasure. I will go away by myself in summer. I will get a job in the daytime. I will: work, work, dare, forget; love and laugh.

I will try to erase the trauma.

SIXTEEN

Aftermath of a Crash

TODAY WHEN A HUGE PASSENGER SHIP crashes it is generally fatal to all aboard, due to its great speed and weight. In the days I write about a pilot had a better chance to live. But I often wondered what a crash did to a man. I've known several who were never the same man again. They lived, but with a screw loose. It was always a very unsettling experience.

Some lost the power of speech (like Richardson, who landed in a tree). Or hearing. Or sex. Others developed an irresponsible streak and became strangers to their friends and family. Some few became religious and disappeared into a seminary. One thing was certain. If the crash was bad enough, there would be a personality change.

My crash was not a bad one. I hit "softly." The ship had lost air speed and therefore was going not more than 50 miles per hour. It was a minimum sample of what a crash can be. I thought I had gotten off scot-free until a stomach pain started showing up about a year later. It acted like an ulcer. Doctors thought it was an ulcer until it wouldn't respond to any of the ulcer treatments.

It was a sharp pain in the pit of the stomach that would come for days at a time, and strong enough to shut out all other earthly considerations. This condition was to be with me, off and on, for the rest of my life. It changed my personality. If it didn't spoil my life, it certainly slowed it down.

When the no-good Standard buried its nose in that hard Texas road, I was wearing a flying belt six inches wide which kept my body from mashing itself against the dashboard. It was a very abrupt stop and an unforgettable yank on my guts. I had no inkling of it but this concentrated violence in the region of my abdomen was to take a lifelong revenge on me.

Recollection: From the 1930s

One year ago this evening as I write, my lips would have been sealed as tight as any R.M.A's[37]—I would sooner confess to felony, theft, murder or even Pro Germanism, than to even a moment of cowardice of the air. But upon its psychology of the thing, let the doctors decide. Now I am again a civilian, then I was—a word of glory—a flyer.

There seems to have been a concerted effort during the war and afterward, on the part of newspapers, fond parents, sweethearts, et al. to make our army aviators out to be supermen and nothing less. I confess that I was not a superman, that I was often as badly scared as a young kitten tied to an unruly kite.

The point is: our so-called supermen were not supermen, not even men, but boys confronted by a tough job which they had to see through. They were frightened, they were scared and they were panicky at times until their souls turned pink—but also, they were more afraid of being "yellow" than of being corpses. They were more afraid of being cowards than of crashing, so wonderous a thing is morale.

Falling through the air a few city blocks, with the acceleration of gravity is a sensation that is exceeded in intensity by nothing. There are no two ways about it—human flesh must quail. For all our vaunted boasting, our "supermen" were panicky, and the flyer who said and acted not was merely putting

---

37 Reserve Military Aviator.

up a brave front. We pilots understood each other pretty well but the general public did not.

Something happened to me after I came to the *Tribune*. Somehow about that time, I lost my nerve and drive, and was content to remain in that job for countless years. Several bad things had happened to me and broke my spirit—my Mother's death and the breakup of our home. Sis's defection. Most of all, my own ill health.

My first five years out of the army I spent money faster than I could make it, trying to get rid of the pain. It was the blackest period of my life. I was in and out of the hospital every six months, to no avail. When the doctors began to put me down as a neurasthenic, a nut, the victim of a fixed idea, I decided to shut up and bear it as best I could. It was my price to pay for the gay adventure of the army and flying.

After the War the world changed. People looked at me differently. Mother died and our old Greenwood home broke up. Then my beloved Sis married the Englishman, went to India and totally disappeared from my life. Girls I knew no longer seemed gay or pleasant. People generally seemed critical. No one understood this damned pain; it changed my life. All from the small crash of a sub-standard Standard which was better off in pieces. The whole thing seemed absurd, but it happened. And there was nothing I could do about it!

I started at the *Tribune* on March 1, 1921. I first worked in Copy and Art. Then Ben McCanna had me transferred to the Business Survey where he was. There I stayed 23 years and 8 months, until October 1944. All those years my salary averaged $75 a week.

McCanna was no ordinary copywriter. He was a connoisseur of the oddities and the excellencies of life, in any period. Though very young, he had a young-old face, thin and gaunt under a very wide forehead. His features were set in a permanent expression of disapproval. He was undoubtedly an intellectual, but a rare one.

He had gone to both Holy Cross and Ignatius but I had never met him until the day he, Leo and I rode in a taxi cab to the LaSalle Street Station to see Leo off for New York, where he had been promoted to publicity director of the *New York News*, a terrific step up. Leo had found McCanna in a mediocre job somewhere and had gotten him his present berth on the *Tribune*. Leo, sad at leaving Chicago, told us to be good friends.

March 29, 1921, Tuesday

Things have gone very well materially since I left off this account of my journal. I am now with the *Chicago Tribune* as a copywriter, in Leo's old job.

In another way things are very wrong. I can't explain it but most of the time I feel so hopeless and spiritless that I would wish to be rid of it all. I came home from work tonight, ate no supper, came into my room and bawled my eyes out for five minutes. This story seems to be a prolonged one of grief. And my only relief is the writing herein.

April 2, 1921, Sunday

The chief value of this diary is going to be as a reminder of the terrific struggle that I waged against the reaction of war, against grief, hopelessness, despair, inertia and physical suffering due to influenza, four operations, nostalgia and loneliness. When I have finally succeeded and won my economic independence I can turn to this book and read of the struggles again.

I have no object in life now but to gain my economic freedom. By that I mean a steady income of about $200 to $300 a month[38] separate from the work I do so that I can feel independent and quit work if I want to, and write. To do this I figure

---

38 Those values of would be equivalent to $3,000 to $4,500 in today's dollars.

on constructing a three-flat building in two years and having it paid for in three.

December 22, 1921, Thursday
Once more I take out the old diary, after a long interval, to put the finishing touch to an old, old tale. In another volume, a more fuller version of this story is told.

On or about October 1, 1921, I left the copy department of the *Tribune* on an extended leave of absence due to ill health, a dejected state of mind that made life intolerable, and home circumstances that were very hard to bear. I went down to Sheridan Beach, Indiana, and built a summer house on a lot I owned there. This took up my time and attention until December 1st. I came home and stayed a week and on Wednesday I embarked for St. Louis.

It was during that visit I came to realize, in a particular moment, that I did not love *her*, but a creature of the imagination that sprang and grew from the knowing of her. I saw her ring—on the engagement finger—while she was eating caviar. A piece of my soul was flying off into eternity of space and time to never return.

The feeling mounted and mounted till I actually regretted so many years that had come to nothing, that had been spoiled and wasted through the knowing of her. With that conviction came a great determination to repair the waste of those years, and the passing of friends that I had let go as inconsequential. She was not the same person as the blue-eyed goddess of South Haven.

I thought of the war and what I had done for her in attempting to prove that I was capable of heroism. I thought of the several times that Death had miraculously passed me by. If I had died, I thought, and could feel myself cold in the grave, would she even think of me?

I thought of the men who had died for other women and

were lying cold and disintegrating from Ypres to the Marne. I thought of the incalculable sacrifice and silliness of which my sex is capable. Many times I had fallen in the air (with a prayer for mercy), many times I had been in situations so terrifying as must stop the heart—for this perfumed, slightly overdressed piece of human flesh.

I wanted laurels and ribbands to lay at her feet. Other men had wanted the same and were dead as the consequence. Why had the merciful Father of men spared me and not them?

December 24, 1921 (Christmas Eve)
There is, I believe, some curse upon our family, if that sort of thing is possible. I had taken a long chance against impossible odds and was beaten. It was logical to die before I reached the last stage of this physical and moral destitution. I could in imagination feel the cold steel against my temple, and there the old agony of living, this deep wide hurt that will not heal would trouble me no more. But what then when it was over—

"Come unto me all ye who labor, grieve and are heavily burdened and I will refresh you." Those words came out of the night to me. For the sake of eternity, I was able to forget the present, Christ seemed to speak to me across the centuries. And I did what I never thought I could do. I took up, again, the thread of life. It was a real spiritual experience.

It was a firm conviction; as God as my judge I realized that during those years I had been in love with a figment of my own imagination, with a non-entity which surpassed the reality. I swear that, numbed and shocked as I was, I realized that there was no love in my heart for Sis Walsh.

SEVENTEEN

The End of Drums

April 2, 1922

It is not too often that a man is overwhelmed by good fortune. I have known so much of ill that the reverse seems a trifle strange. In the last twenty-four hours I was offered a job as advertising manager of a manufacturing plant in Ohio, at a salary of $7,000 a year. And I was nominated for a job in the publicity department of the *Tribune*. Remuneration unknown, but experience excellent. It means a chance to know personally McCormick and Patterson, owners of the *Tribune*, also Thomason, Parsons and Cleary. And to work with one of the boys I like best, Ben McCanna.

Three days ago Art Stringer asked me to be his partner in an enterprise in California. Last night Norma Schulte presented me with a finely made handkerchief; the thought behind making it means a lot to me. And Broadfuehrer said today that he was going to bring down some bulbs for me to plant at the Grey Duck (my cottage). Today at lunch Tom Scanlon told me he would rather be in business with me than with the man he is now tied up with.

And finally, Englehardt told Broadfuehrer that an ad I wrote two weeks ago sold over a hundred thousand dollars' worth of business. Broadfuehrer asked him to give him a note to that effect so that he could show it to Parsons and it would be in the record when the time came for me to get a raise.

O Lady Luck, you are smiling on me!

The End of Drums

I was very new at the new job when, sitting at my desk in the Business Survey Department, located on one of the top floors of the old *Tribune* building,[39] the newspaper clipping of Sis Walsh's engagement to the Englishman came across my desk. I felt that day as though somebody had knocked the wind out of me. I could not work. I could not think. I sat at my desk staring at the wall ahead, for I don't know how long. I felt as though my life were over and nothing left.

How was I to get through the rest of my life? I felt that for all intents and purposes it was over. A profound melancholy enveloped me. I did not believe in suicide. The Irish never do. I felt that the mainspring of my life was broken. The love thing had touched my life to the quick.

At the same time, I could see clearly that a life with Sis had never been in the cards. I could see clearly the motives of all the people involved, and they were honorable. I could not blame anybody but myself. I had tilted at an impossible windmill and failed comically.

Sis, for all the enchantment she had held for me, was really a very matter-of-fact, prosy, ambitious person. She had turned out big, good-looking, and not at all the cute little beach gamine I had known. I was a poor, aspiring nobody who had thought to win her with a fine war record. David, the attractive Englishman, well connected by family in London and Calcutta, stood for an exciting life in the highest social circles of a great empire.

Sis, since she had metamorphosed into the adult Sis, was

---

39 The building at Dearborn and Madison; this event occurred prior to the building of the famous Tribune Tower.

very keen on society and on moving in the right circles. After all, it was by sheerest accident that she and I had ever met in the mellow old fishing village of South Haven where her family had gone slumming for two summers because Pop's business was in a depression. So why should she give her poor-boy admirer aviator a second thought? No reason. And she didn't.

Long ago I forgave her for what she did to my life. I put it down as an accident of Fate and laissez-faire economics. Or was it simple-minded stupidity that she couldn't hear our genes screaming for union, and that I couldn't accept the situation. But now I could coast; I had almost persuaded myself that I could roll with the punch.

Shall I ever forget the Saturday morning Sis was being married to the Englishman in St. Louis? It was a handsome society wedding, by all accounts. I had an invitation, of course, but declined. I was at the Business Survey Department, sitting at my desk on one of the top floors of the old Tribune building. I couldn't work. I just sat there and stared at the blank wall in front of me for I don't know how long. (This blank staring had become almost a habit.)

"What's the matter with you, Corbett? You sick?"

Ben McCanna, sitting at the next desk, had apparently been watching me. He came over, put a friendly arm across my shoulder, and said:

"You've been staring at that wall for the last fifteen minutes, and giving me the willies."

He put his hand to his chin and thought for a minute.

"I've got it!" he exclaimed. "Yessir, that's it! You need to meet new people. You need to find a gal! Today. We'll start with lunch. I've a date at the Russian Tea Room. You can tag along. It'll be a good start."

Coming toward us, through Chicago's smog, on Michigan Avenue, was a colorful, nay, a gorgeous bit of femininity, -tawny blonde hair in a luxuriant bob, very blue eyes wide apart, fair complexion and a Norman-Irish cast of features. A melancholy smile, withal.

More noticeable than all the rest was her youth and vivacity. She was charm and outgoingness personified. This whirlwind of joie de vivre was in perfect taste, expensively clothed. She would be a smash with anything male, but she fitted Ben McCanna perfectly, and his exotic connoisseurship of all that was the unusual and best. She was especially made for him, I thought.

She greeted Ben, enthusiastically, and was overflowing with bits of news and gossip of arty people and struggling writers. She knew everybody and all their goings-on. She was articulate, expressed herself better than well, -charmingly. I judged she must be a top society writer for one of its papers. She was all eyes and attention to Ben and seemed fascinated with his male gauntness and period face. She hardly noticed me but I didn't mind. I kept thinking, how wonderful for Ben.

We proceeded to the Russian Tea Room, past its gargantuan doorman, and the three of us had lunch. I was hardly noticed, and felt like an intruder in an intimate scene. Ben himself seemed overwhelmed by the avalanche of words and charm. It might have been just another lunch, in a faked Russian setting with a bookish fellow, his girl and an intruding friend. I find the scene hard to remember in detail or to describe.

I didn't know it but it was right here, for me, that the drums of war stopped sounding. I did not realize it at the time, but in that moment JN-4Ds, silver wings, engine lore and bumpy flying fields faded.

Here my life took a near turn and new interests in a new milieu, -the field of writing and newspapering. Henceforth the scene and setting of my efforts was to be the great newspaper, the greatest in the country next to the *New York Times*. And greater than it, in the opinion of some.

But if I could in that moment have foreseen the future

accurately, I would certainly have gathered my duffel and run away. When Ben gave me Nancy, it all changed.

The End

Cy Corbett's Cast of Characters

Brief Description and Relationship to the Author

Family

"Cy": Thomas Cyril Corbett (1895–1976)
   The author of this autobiography.
   b. Chicago, Illinois. Died, Benton Harbor, Michigan.

"Mother": Elizabeth "Lizzie" Frances (Keenan) Corbett (1865–1919)
   b. Albany, New York. Raised in LaPorte, Indiana, came to Chicago about 1886. Widow, mother of three. After her husband died, she gathered up all assets (a house and a little insurance) and bought a six-apt. building at 6318-20 Greenwood Ave.

"Father": Thomas Henry Corbett, (1864–1904)
   b. New Orleans. Worked for N.B. Holden Shoe Company. Died at 39.

"Aunty": Therese Marie Keenan (1862–1927)
   Spinster, b. Albany, New York. 1862. Elkhart & La Porte, Indiana. Came to Chicago about 1882. Occupation: dressmaker for fashionable clients. Had own small shop.

"Marie": Elizabeth Marie Corbett (1899–1969)
   My sister, who married Vincent Cunningham.

"Buster": Thomas Harold Corbett (1904–1973)
My brother. After the death of Vincent Cunningham (husband of Marie Corbett), Tom took over the Cunningham Glass Washer business, which Vince had started.

"Spot": the Corbett family dog

"Uncle Will": William J. Corbett (1872–1948)
Will had worked with my father at the Holden Shoe Company. Later he owned the C.W. Mark's Shoe Company, Chicago. Residence: 1430 Lakeshore Drive. Was a member of Notre Dame University's Associate Board of Lay Trustees and a director of Milwaukee Road Railroad.

"Aunt Nora": Sister Nora M. Benedicta Corbett (1869–1936)
My aunt who became a Catholic nun of the Mercy Order. Sister Benedicta taught school at All Saint's Parish at Twenty-Fifth Street and Wallace Avenue.

"Aunt Kate": Catherine M. Corbett (1858–1944)
She was the first of nine children born to James Dore Corbett and Mary Bridget O'Connor. Her father died when she was only 16 years old. To help support the family, she worked in a hat factory, a sweat shop.

Grandma Corbett (1842–1928)
Mary Bridget O'Connor Corbett, born in Ireland. Married James Dore Corbett, of County Limerick, Ireland, in Chicago, then moved to New Orleans. Following the death of her husband in 1874 she moved the family back to Chicago.

Extended Family

Vincent Cunningham (1895–1941)
   Classmate, St. Ignatius Class of 1918. He lived on Chicago's North Side (Greenleaf Avenue), and had a great interest in mechanics. He married my sister, Marie, in 1922.

Annis Cunningham
   Sister of Vincent Cunningham, and friend of Marie Corbett. My group of friends often socialized with the Cunninghams. Vince drove them around in his Mercer automobile, which was quite a novelty.

Childhood Friends & Neighborhood People

Chet Herrod (1895–1946)
   Returned from World War I a hero and married my friend Louise Jefferson.

Doherty, Lt. Godson of Mrs. Reynolds (Ned's mother)

Kearns, Frank Reed (1897–1979)
   Classmate at St. Rita's. Had younger brother, George. His father then was a pale, trembling alcoholic. His mother, a large but permanently upset woman, worked in order to keep the family together. Frank had a brilliant and penetrating mind with a bent to the sciences. Intelligent.

King, Earl D. (1894–1942)
   St. Ignatius Class of 1915. Lived at 6529 Greenwood Avenue, Woodlawn. He was a member of our tennis foursome. He and Ned were always partners against Toots and me. We played matches about every day, after school, in good weather, on the courts in Jackson Park, and on our own Court on Greenwood Avenue, across the street from our house. After St. Ignatius Earl

put in a year at University of Chicago Law School, but decided he didn't like it. He left for the War in September, 1917, and saw a great deal of action in the Tank Corps. Earl had two sisters, one of whom became a nun. Earl was rather shy and reticent and I never knew his family, incredible as it may seem now. He was a great reader and had a bit of a flair for writing.

McCormick, Joe
   Woodlawn boy, friend of Dorothy Lyons.

Murphy, J. Sherwin (1896–1971)
   St. Ignatius Class of 1918. Lived at 4821 Dorchester Avenue. Childhood friend. Sherwin worked in advertising and later became a skilled amateur photographer. Some of his work is in the Chicago History Museum. A lifelong bachelor who kept in sporadic contact, often visiting me. Sherwin died alone in Manistee, Michigan.

Reynolds, Edward "Ned" Dore (1895–1974)
   St. Ignatius Class of 1916. My oldest childhood and lifelong friend who lived in Woodlawn. Ned's father, Benjamin F. Reynolds, died young. Ned was raised by his mother and grandmother, Mrs. Dore. Ned left Woodlawn in the fall of 1916 for the Seminary at Florissant, Missouri. An exemplar to our family and neighborhood of correct conduct, of scholarly and cultural attainments. The only child of Ellen Dore Reynolds.

"Mrs. Reynolds": Reynolds, Ellen Dore (1858–1938)
   Mother of my good friend Ned Reynolds.

Shane, Jim
   Contact who was in the naval reserves.

Sheehan, Tom
   An old school friend.

Wideman Family
Neighborhood family who lived at 6314 Greenwood Avenue.

Wideman, Mrs. Mary Hogan (1870–1940)
She was viewed as the neighborhood busybody. The family summered in South Haven at the same time as the Corbett family.

Wideman, Alfred (1900–1968)
Alfred took several of the photos in South Haven, in 1911 and 1912. In 1941 Alfred was an advertising artist. At the time of his death he was the organist for two Catholic churches.

Weisenburger, Arnold "Toots" V. (1895–1993)
Woodlawn neighbor, the youngest from a large family of 4 girls and 3 boys. I first knew Toots in 8th grade at Holy Cross. He at once attached himself to our family, was always underfoot, and shortly became "sweet" on Marie, who was never able to take him seriously. From 8th grade on there were very few family events that did not include Toots. He was a pious boy, went to Mass and Communion every day, but religion cast no damper on his ebullient spirits. He had a deep common sense about both religion and money, and seemed to enjoy life thoroughly. However bright-minded he was by nature he always curiously played the fool, either to entertain or to accentuate an absurd situation such as the time, at a dance, he argued religion with the Episcopal minister.

Girl Friends & Families

Glaser, Anna-Marie (1899–1970)
Nashville, Tennessee. Friend of Cunningham family who had attended boarding school with Annis. She often visited Chicago, -she and I became lifelong friends.

Jefferson, Louise Gaiennie (1898–1928)
    Lived at 5143 Ingleside Avenue, Hyde Park. Very "Frenchish." When Chet Herrod proposed to her after returning from the War, she asked me what she should do. She gave the impression that she was more interested in me than Chet, but I wasn't receptive. She married Chet in 1920 and died in childbirth eight years later.

Jefferson, Ralph
    Brother of Louise Jefferson.

Lyons, Dorothy (1900–unknown)
    Her family lived in a very fine 6-apt. building at 6115-17 Greenwood Avenue, about two blocks north of us. Mr. Lyons, her father, had been for some years connected with the police department. The first time I remember seeing Dorothy was on the tennis courts at Jackson Park. Ned, Earl, Toots and I were playing out one of our heroic matches. I asked Toots who she was. He said I ought to know her, that she had gone to Holy Cross. After the match he introduced us.
    I thought of her for several days, not seeing her again, and my thoughts resulted in the poem, "The sky today is as opal here." I am uncertain as to when I saw her again and can't find it in the Diary—but think Toots arranged it, as he was a great matchmaker. She married fellow University of Chicago student Thomas Stevenson Rogers (1898–1972) and moved to Washington, D.C.

Schulte, Norma (1899–1982)
    The first girl I ever took out. A friend of Marie's. I believe we met the family in South Haven. Her father was a prosperous druggist with a store at 55th Street and Kimbark Avenue. They lived in a nice home at 54th and Kimbark. Norma was small, dark with sloe eyes and rather French—vivacious and chic. She

had all the latest expressions and fashions and was something of a coquette. She had, I think, a crush on me but in those days I could never see any girl seriously except Sis Walsh.

Lillian "Sis" Walsh and Family

"Sis": Lillian I. Walsh (1900–1969)

The blue-eyed goddess, of St. Louis. I met her first in old South Haven, in 1911. Her family was staying at "the Dewey," a neighboring and much more snooty resort than "Sleepy Hollow." She and her brother Rob and I practically spent the summers of 1911 and 1912 together. She was not particularly good-looking or beautiful, but had an indefinable charm and personality. Whatever it was she had, I wanted, and fell head over heels in love with her.

"Rob": Robert. P. Walsh (1898–1964)

A large, soft-spoken and matter-of-fact fellow but a fine, humorous companion. An accomplished musician, even in those days, but did not seem to care for anything else—even his father's profession, much to the concern of his mother. We built a canoe together in 1911. His father furnished the money for the canvas covering. It worked! The next year we put a sail on it. Bob became an architect but was never the success his father and grandfather were. He had no money sense.

"Mom Walsh": Grace Pollard Walsh (1880–1971)
Of 5959 Cabanne Pl., St. Louis.

Robert W. Walsh, Sr. (1855–1928)
Of 5959 Cabanne Pl., St. Louis, partner in architectural firm.

College Friends

Beckman, William E., M.D. (1898–1977)
   Classmate, St. Ignatius Class of 1918. Became a doctor.

Colnon, Edward A. (L.) (1897–1970)
   St. Ignatius Class of 1918. The richest boy in our class was Ed Colnon (his family, of course). They had one of the early automobiles and used to take Fr. Mullens for a ride every so often, around the city or maybe to a neighboring town. He became a Jesuit Priest. (Editor's Note: *Loyola University Magazine* lists him as Edward A., while all other records have him listed as Edward L.)

McGivena, Leo E. (1896–1980)
   St. Ignatius Class of 1916. Leo was editor of *Loyola University Magazine* when I was first published. Later, in the army years, I gave him a wild motorcycle ride in Texas. Leo worked at *Chicago Tribune*, and helped me land my job there. He also introduced me to Ben McCanna. Leo moved to New York to work on the *Tribune's* sister paper, the *New York Daily News*. There, he developed the widely known "Tell It To Sweeny" advertising campaign. Later, he began his own advertising agency. Leo corresponded with me often.

Ryan, John
   Classmate at St. Ignatius. John was in Aviation also, and came over to my house to practice Morse Code.

Ryan, Marc
   Classmate at St. Ignatius. Involved with the *Loyola University Magazine*.

Walsh, Sinon J. (1896–1938)
St. Ignatius Class of 1918. I am thinking of his spunky courage. Dead at an early age. I see his clear defiance of the world as organized, and his willingness to die rather than to himself change.

Walsh, Tom
Classmate at St. Ignatius.

St. Ignatius Faculty

Mr. Claude M. Bakewell, S.J. (1892–1921)
A scholar and teacher of Greek. Brilliant scholar of the Greek dramatists. Had him for Greek two years in college, the *Antigone*. Not yet ordained. When he read Greek to class it sounded like spoken music, like nothing I had ever heard. He was transferred about the time I left for the army. Several letters from him. He died of a burst appendix off in a rustic camp in the woods, away from medical attention, still unordained, about 1920.

Rev. Charles Coppens, S.J. (1835–1920)
Professor of French, History of Philosophy, and Religion. Born in Belgium, died in Chicago at age 85. 67 years as a Jesuit. On my way to the army he gave me *A Soldier's Diary* and his blessing.

Rev. John Baptist Furay, S.J. (1873–1952)
President of St. Ignatius College. He was a very cold and withdrawn man, and seldom smiled. I thought him overly pious. And that he suffered much from over conscientiousness. He was hard on himself and everybody else. He was president of the University.

Arnold Joseph Garvy, S.J. (1868–1950)

Librarian and Professor of English. English professor in College. Best teacher I ever had. My first encounter with a truly liberal mind. Irish and Scotch. Family lived in Holy Name Parish during its heyday. Lived to 86. Champion of the Negroes. A lifelong personal friend. Converted Dorothy (my wife). He is the Arnold in our son Billy's name (William Arnold Corbett).

George J. Leahey, S.J. (1867–1928)

Vice President, Prefect of Studies and Discipline. A kindly, greying man. Prefect of discipline. Never had him in class. He had a very fatherly feeling towards Toots and me. Forgave us innumerable tardinesses. I still see him very vividly. In no way distinguished but full of love and affection for the boys. Miscast as a disciplinarian. When he died years later his sister phoned me at the *Tribune*. He had asked that I be one of his pallbearers. I was, and am very touched. And remembered that one time he said he wished I could have been his son.

Father William P. Lyons, S.J. (1863–1928)

Professor of Political Economy. Founder of Loyola University Press.

Eugene A. Magevney, S.J. (1855–1919)

Professor of History. Served as president of Creighton University from 1908 until the summer of 1914 before returning to St. Ignatius, where he had previously served as Vice President. He was short, heavyset, spoke deliberately, had a large aquiline nose, and generally conducted himself as how we imagined a Roman senator would. We privately referred to him as "The Old Roman."

Mr. Austin G. Schmidt, S.J. (1883–1960)

English Literature and English Composition. I'll always remember his talk on Dr. Samuel Johnson, the Oxford scholar and lexicographer. Schmidt was slight, dark and full of electricity. His mind was clear and sharp as a razor.

Father Patrick J. Lomasney, S.J. (1876–1944)
Born in Ireland, I asked him if he had a cure for melancholy. He said no, but suggested friends, books, diversions. Before leaving for the war he gave me some beautiful hand-painted scapulars.

Father Mathery
From Florissant; he gave me a crucifix when I was in the army; I used it at Mother's deathbed.

Acquaintances During Air Service Years

Adams
Love Field flight instructor.

Becker, Lt.
Cadet who bunked next to me at Aviation Ground School.

Bisbinghoff
Cadet at Love Field. Known as the unluckiest man on the field. Involved in a midair collision with Mead Terry.

Croarkin, Paul C. (1891–1951)
I knew the family when they lived at 6336 Woodlawn Avenue, Chicago. Mr. Croarkin, an attorney, made a killing in grain and the family moved to Edgewater by 1920 (6317 Winthrop Avenue). Paul, like his father, was an attorney. He was instrumental in my joining the Army Air Corps. Tragedy befell the family after their youngest son, Harold, was convicted of murdering a six-year-old boy with a hammer in 1927.

Campbell, Lt. William T.
　Flight instructor at Love Field.

Castle, Vernon (1887–1918)
　Royal Air Force pilot who died in a Texas flying accident. He was famous as a dancer along with his wife, Irene Castle. He was born in Norwich, England, as Vernon William Blythe. An entertainer, he changed his last name to Castle after arriving in the United States.

Chance, Frank
　Played his fiddle, "Mighty Lak' A Rose" in Air Camp.

Cunningham, Col.
　Love Field. Bright young engineer-designer who had been a professor at MIT.

de Gozzaldi
　Cadet at Love Field. Known as "The Duke." Born in Austria, a graduate of Harvard. After the war he worked as a solicitor for the *Dallas News*.

De Learie
　Cadet who had crashed many times without a scratch.

Dewey, John P.
　Love Field, editor, *Love Field Loops*.

Dodd, Captain
　Love Field. The officer in charge of flying.

Cecil, Dodge
　Captain, and excellent flyer. I flew with him one day and met him the next day in the hospital, where we spent ten days recovering from the flu.

Covington
Cadet from Covington, Kentucky, who won the craps game on the train to Camp Dick.

Eastman
A flyer I met in New York. Banker, I think, with Chemical National.

Emerie
Love Field. Went on a joy ride with Harrison and they got tangled up in a high tension electric line. I was supposed to go, but couldn't find my goggles.

Faneuf, Abie
Cadet at Love Field. Good natured Yankee. Unusual erratic flyer. When Abie "took off," everyone else came down. He became a chemist out East.

Finsterwald
Cadet at Love Field. Spun down 400 feet and smashed up in a chicken yard.

Fisher, Ewing "Bud" (1895–1978)
From Springfield, Illinois. Cadet at Love Field, became a lifelong friend. Introduced me to social life in Dallas.

Fisher, Floyd Clayton "Bud" (1895–1961)
From Patterson, Pennsylvania. I was introduced to him just after he recently crashed. Bud was holding his broken nose on the way to the hospital, telling me, "Made a rather bad landing."

Fitzgerald, Roy
Harwood White's pal and buddy at Ground School.

Foote, Henry
Love Field. A civilian flight instructor, rated by the men as a "nervous Nellie." Short, heavyset and gruff.

Goetz, Captain
Love Field. A Kiwi, lawyer, and the most hated man I'd ever seen.

Gray, Leslie R.
Cadet at Love Field. Was an instructor at U. of Illinois, always seemed to be reading a scientific journal.

Harrison
Asked me to go on a joy ride, but I didn't have my goggles. He took Emerie instead, and they got tangled up in a high tension electric line.

Hefron, Lt. Buck
A flying fool.

Herrin, Cadet
Love Field. Soldier of fortune, and originator of base Potato Bug Races.

Insinger, John
Cadet from Greenleaf, Colorado, killed at Love Field April 9, 1918, when two machines crashed about five hundred feet in the air.

Jewett, Lt. W.A.
Met him in New York. Suggested we fly for a Chinese warlord after being discharged.

Kern
Cadet in Ground School.

Lehrbas, Lloyd "Larry"
Love Field. Associate editor, *Love Field Loops*. Became a famous war correspondent and later an aid to General McArthur. We stayed in touch after the war.

Lutz, Dave
Cadet at Love Field. A glutton for flying.

McKeever, James L.
Second Lt., of New York City. Killed with John Widenham when their airplane went into a slide and crashed, about 20 miles north of Fort Worth. Accident resulted from a straight nosedive, as though the horizontal controls were snapped. We marched in the funerals.

McLaughlin, Dallas
Widow, friend of Bud Fisher.

Mulvahill, Marshall
Suitor of Pet Thorton, Dallas socialite, friend of Bud Fisher.

Murphy, Ralph
My bunkie at ground school.

Netherwood, Major
I saw him crash in Love Field while I was talking with a sentry.

O'Connell, Major
Love Field; the commandant. A good-natured Irishman.

Reeves, J. Fred
Jesuit educated, a flyer with captain's bars and a crushed English cap. Saw him on a train to Long Island.

Regan, Dick
    One of the St. Ignatius boys who joined the British Flying Corps.

Requa
    Love Field. A civilian flight instructor, a Frenchman, a beau exquisite.

Redmond
    Sergeant at Love Field.

Richmond, (first name unknown)
    Cadet who caught on fire, crashed into the only tree in a field.

Richardson
    Cadet who lost the power of speech after a crash.

Russell, Lt.
    Love Field. Flew with him "to hunt some birds" (downed planes). While with him he performed some "strictly forbidden" stunts.

Suter, Lt.
    Love Field. Crashed and broke his leg.

Terry, Mead
    Cadet who survived a midair collision with Bisbinghoff.

Thorton, Peg
    Dallas socialite, friend of Bud Fisher.

Wenban, Bob
    I knew him from the Air Service. Later helped me obtain job at Lyon & Healy.

White, Harwood
   Met in Ground School. He was the brother of noted writer Stewart Edward White.

Widenham, John M.
   Of Los Angeles, California. Killed with James McKeever when their airplane went into a slide and crashed, about 20 miles north of Fort Worth. Accident resulted from a straight nosedive, as though the horizontal controls were snapped. We marched in the funerals.

Williams, Sgt.
   Love Field drill sergeant

Williamson
   Cadet of 136 Squadron. I walked to N.C.O. club with him and talked 'till late.

Zinn, Earl
   Cadet who was involved in the air collision that killed Insinger at Love Field in 1918. He was mistakenly taken to the morgue and thought dead.

Work Acquaintances

Steger Piano

Hayes, Lambert K. (1892–1942)
   St. Ignatius Class of 1915. Son of Chicago surgeon Dr. Patrick Hayes. Worked at Steger & Sons Piano Company; twice elected Municipal Court Judge, Chicago; announcer on a weekly religious radio program. Served in U.S. Navy, 1917. Was instrumental in helping me obtain my first job after my discharge from the Army Air Corps.

Byrne, Charles E. (1887–1958)
St. Ignatius Class of 1906; LL.B. 1916. Was the advertising manager and sales manager for Steger & Sons Piano Company, 1911–1919; Vice President and General Manager 1919–1930, after which he had a private law practice. He was elected Superior Court Judge and served for 13 years prior to his death.

Duffy, Edward J. (1895–1971)
St. Ignatius Class of 1917. 1920 US Census says he worked for a "piano firm," which was Steger's. In the 1940 census he was listed as an accountant, living with his mother, Catherine. He was godfather to my third son. Upon the death of Ed's mother in 1958, I served as pallbearer along with fellow classmate Jim Mangan.

Adams
Salesman at the Steger Piano Company.

Lowenthal
Salesman at the Steger Piano Company.

Chicago Journal of Commerce

Borhn, José
Grey-haired Cuban, editor of *Chicago Journal of Commerce.*

Hoyne, Maclay
Illinois state's attorney, whom I interviewed for *Chicago Journal of Commerce.*

Martin, Paul
Drama critic, wrote book reviews.

McMillan, Capt.
    Fellow worker, *Chicago Journal of Commerce.*

Russell, Capt.
    Fellow worker, *Chicago Journal of Commerce.*

Chicago Tribune

Brodfuehrer, Oscar (1889–1962)
    Tribune manager of Copy & Art dept.

Cleary, James (1886–1972)
    Head of *Tribune's* Copy & Art. My boss in 1923. According to his obituary, Cleary came to the *Tribune* in 1907 as a reporter. He was involved in founding *The New York Daily News* in 1919, and then returned to the *Tribune.*

Macfarlane, Wilbert E. "Bert" (1882–1944)
    Tribune business manager at the time of his death at age 62. Was one of the friendlier managers.

McCanna, Ben (1899–1937)
    Friend from *Tribune* years. Married Clare Foy, an artist. Moved to NYC. Ben died there.

McCormick, Col. Robert.
    Publisher of the *Chicago Tribune.*

Patterson, J.M.
    Owner of the *Chicago Tribune.*

Thomason, S.E. (1883–1944)

Former *Tribune* business manager who left the paper in 1927 to buy the *Tampa Tribune*, later founded the *Chicago Daily Times* in 1929. He died in March 1944 at age 61.

Stringer, Art

In 1922 he asked me to be his partner in an enterprise in California.

ABOUT THE AUTHOR

Thomas Cyril "Cy" Corbett (1895–1976) grew up in Chicago's South Side neighborhood of Woodlawn, in an Irish-Catholic family. Along with his younger sister and brother, Cy was raised by his widowed mother and her sister. A serious student from a young age, he attended St. Ignatius (Loyola University) for high school and college. At the outbreak of World War I Cy enlisted in the US Army Air Corps. In training, he experienced sixteen forced landings and one serious crash, which likely contributed to a painful abdominal ailment that affected him for the rest of his life.

(Photo by Sherwin Murphy)

In 1921 he joined the *Chicago Tribune* as a copywriter in their business department, and was instrumental in creating advertisements promoting the opening of the Tribune Tower in 1925.

He continued at the *Tribune* with various writing and editing assignments. Additionally, in 1932 he began to write freelance articles, short stories, and a novel in his spare time. In the mid-1930s he achieved some notoriety with nonfiction and biographical articles, printed mainly in specialty publications and the *Loyola Alumnus Magazine*. Success with his fictional pieces, however, eluded him.

He resigned from the *Tribune* in 1944, retired to Michigan, and built a small summer resort where he lived until his death at age eighty.

Throughout his life he kept journals, which he used to make sense of the events of the day. They provided him an avenue to record general observations about life and the people he knew. They were also a therapy to cope with bouts of depression, which he called "The Irish Melancholy."

In 1970 he began writing reminiscences of his neighborhood and early years. These are presented in another volume of the *Cy Corbett Chronicles*.

ABOUT THE EDITOR:

William Arnold Corbett (1947–) is the youngest of Cy Corbett's three sons. Born in Chicago, from age two he lived at his parents' summer resort in southwestern Michigan.

In 1969 he graduated from the University of Michigan with a degree in journalism, working in that field ten years as both a newspaper reporter and freelance writer and photographer. In 1980 he switched careers to become a financial advisor, but his interest in writing continued. His nonfiction book on ethical money management, *Financial Guide for Catholics*, was published in 1989.

When his father was on his deathbed, he promised to look after the journals. After his mother died in 1981, Bill began a forty-year process of transcribing the handwritten volumes, organizing them into logical order and creating very readable works that describe the modern world from the point of view of someone born in 1895.

Made in the USA
Middletown, DE
28 March 2023